HISTORY OF
EDUCATION
IN ICELAND

A Glacial River of Iceland

HISTORY OF EDUCATION
IN ICELAND

BY

GEORGE T. TRIAL

CAMBRIDGE
W. HEFFER & SONS LTD

First Published - - 1945

2181

Printed and Bound in Great Britain at the Works of
W. HEFFER AND SONS LTD., CAMBRIDGE, ENGLAND

Acknowledgments

The aid received from Icelandic scholars and educators has been of great value to me. At no time were they too busy to give interviews, information and valuable suggestions. The author extends most grateful thanks to all those who helped in the gathering of the data. In particular, great appreciation is extended to Jakob Kristinsson, Director of Public Education; Freysteinn Gunnarson, Headmaster of the Teachers' Training School; Helgi Tryggason, member of the Teachers' Training School staff; S. Thorlacius, Headmaster of the largest of the three elementary schools in Reykjavik; Jon Sigurdsson, Headmaster of Laugarneskolinn; Palmi Hannesson, Headmaster of the Grammar School in Reykjavik; Fridereik Olafsson, Headmaster of the Navigation School; M. E. Jessen, Headmaster of the Marine Engineers' School; G. Rosinkranz, Headmaster of the Co-operative Society Commercial School; B. P. Kalman; Helgi Eiriksson, Headmaster of the Technical School, and Soren Sorenson. All the above-mentioned men have been most interested. Soren Sorenson has been the chief technical adviser and interpreter, and has given much inspiration and helpful guidance in the writing of this book.

Preface

Previously to the present change in international affairs the island of Iceland was merely a tiny spot on the world map, of little importance; economically, strategically, or otherwise.

On the big stage of history, where the scene is constantly changing and dramatic events occur in rapid succession, the unexpected had happened: This "insignificant" island had become an important strategic point in the allied line of defence. Iceland had come to the fore almost overnight. It had come out of obscurity to appear in the front-page news of our newspapers.

Webster's dictionary informs us that the island of Iceland lies in the north Atlantic Ocean and belongs properly to the Western Hemisphere. Says Webster: "The great importance of Iceland as a country lies in the old Norse stock here displayed in its purest and best development. The language and spirit of the race are expressed in an interesting literature. At the time when America was unknown, poets and story-tellers and historians flourished in Iceland. Poems and that peculiar form of epic called the Saga abounded before there was any extensive English literature."

Frankly, I had never paid much attention to this far-away country. America was enough for me. Then came this drastic change; sudden and unexpected. I found myself on the way to this outpost of defence—and civilization—to this old Saga-Island, with its peculiar name of Ice-land. To see this volcanic island, covered with ice and snow, rise out of the ocean one nasty cold winter morning was really an imposing, but not very inspiring sight. One is tempted to agree with the old Viking, Hrafnafloki, who gave the country its chilly name. The cold wind blowing from the north which seems to penetrate right through the marrow and have a hypotensive effect upon one's mental functions, makes one wonder what could tempt human beings to inhabit such a rocky island where infernal fires are burning underneath a cap of ice. However, when one steps ashore in Reykjavik, the capitol of Iceland, a surprise is in store.

As the chilly feeling, caused by the raw north wind and by the first impression of the country from a distance, begins to wear off, one realizes that the air is not as cold as expected. The mental outlook becomes more cheerful. Here, in the middle of the winter, close to the Arctic Circle, one would naturally expect an Arctic storm howling or a blizzard blowing.　But the climate does not seem to be at all harsh.　Fur-clad persons are nowhere to be seen.　Men and women, old and young, are walking along the streets in their summer clothes.　The winter sun is shining and the mountains in the distance look beautiful in their winter dress.　I have been here for six months and the winter has, so far, been quite mild.　I am told that there are evidences that the climate is getting warmer.　The big glaciers, Vatnajokull, for instance, are decreasing.

Although the climate is improving, the winters are terribly long and dreary.　The winter days are short and the sun is low in the sky.　The Icelanders, who are industrious people, have availed themselves of modern things.　They have electricity to brighten up the long winter nights.　Progress is everywhere in evidence, progress which is a direct outcome of democratic liberty.

Table of Contents

Charts and Maps

Illustrations

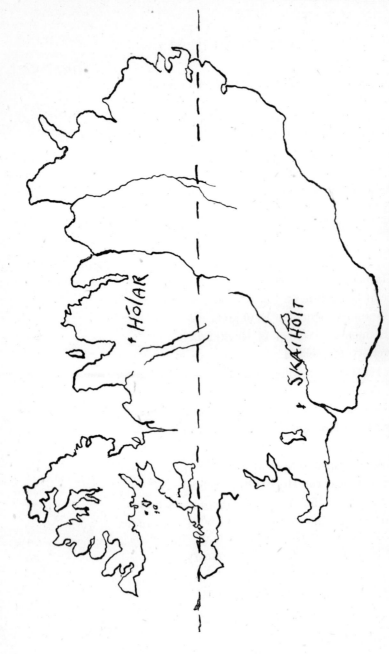

HÓLAR

SKÁLHOLT

Seats of the first Bishoprics and two schools of Iceland

PART I

The Cultural and Literary Advancement of Iceland by Centuries

9TH CENTURY 775–925.
VIKING PERIOD.

Religion based on mythical characters, Odin and Thor.
Part of mythological poems of older *Edda* composed.
Rune letter inscriptions in wood, stone and metal.

10TH CENTURY 903–1030.
SAGA PERIOD. THE HISTORY CENTURY.

930—Parliament founded.
The Althing was the holy centre of the nation where men and women gathered in order to seek instruction and culture.
Poets stayed with the kings to put the story of the king's exploits into poetry. At meetings, sports were held: horse fights, foot races, glimur, etc.

11TH CENTURY 1030–1152.

Christianity introduced by Gissur Hviti and Hjalti Skeggjason at the Althing.
Foreign bishops came to train priests to spread Christianity.
The meetings of the Althing in the spring and autumn were the basis of all Icelandic culture at this period. All events that took place in between were discussed and passed on.
In the schools of this period the subjects taught were:

Reading.	Theology.
Writing.	Making hymns in Latin.
Singing of Masses.	

12TH CENTURY.
THE PEACE PERIOD.

1204—Bishop's seat and school established at Holar.
Schools also started in Odda and Haukadal.
1207—First book written which was a law book, *Vigslodi* (Way to the Fighting).
Arni, the learned, writes the history of the Norwegian Kings and a short history of the Icelanders up to this period.

Cloisters were established at several places in the country but
fell into disrepute soon afterward.

From this time documents and books were written on parchment.

13TH CENTURY 1152–1262.

STURLUNGA PERIOD.

1170–1230—Most Icelandic Sagas written. Snorri Sturluson
wrote *Heimskringla* and *Edda*. Superstition began to grow.

14TH CENTURY 1262–1400.

PERIOD OF NORWEGIAN KINGS.

Icelanders wrote the Chronicle of Norwegian Kings.

Happenings began to be recorded in the form of stories concerning
actual people, but with much romance added.

Then romantic tales of western Europe were brought over.

New style of Saga writing, "Lying Saga." Fictional.

15TH CENTURY 1400–1550.

PERIOD OF THE POWER OF THE CHURCH.

Culture of this period was concerned with hymns, both religious
and fictional.

Fairy tales and rhymes.

Decline of old Nordic literature.

Book printing begun.

16TH CENTURY.

PERIOD OF MONARCHY.

Rule of Norwegian Kings.

A school was founded at Holar in 1652 and at Skalholt in 1653.
The main subjects in this school were Latin, Greek and
Theology.

Translation of the Bible from German.

17TH CENTURY.

Contrast: Much superstition and witchery during this period,
among the common people; but the beginning of scientific
writing by learned men.

Passion psalms by Hallgrimur Petursson.

Collecting of parchments and old literature.

18TH CENTURY.

Monarchy and monopoly.
Outstanding men, such as Arni Magnusson and Pall Vidalin, work hard for civilization.
Eggert Olafsson and Bjarni Palsson worked much for the sciences and civilization.
Rules given as to how and what children shall be taught.
Societies: Icelandic Scientifical, 1729.
Society (Icelandic) for Public Education, 1794.

19TH CENTURY 1750–1918.

National feeling grows and a fight for liberty begins.
Literary Society founded.
The National Library is started.
Now the civilization grows and many people who have learned abroad come back with new opinions. Agricultural Schools for men and women are founded.
Household schools, adult schools, newspapers and journals begin.

20TH CENTURY.

University and special schools founded.
Great advance in the arts, and interest is aroused in the theatre.
Moving pictures and sports (new) are introduced.

Table of Events

A.D.

870—Harald, the fairhair, ruled Norway and forced many people who wished to remain free chieftains to flee the country, many came to Iceland.

871—The Norwegian chiefs, Ingolfur and Hjorleifur, land in Iceland for permanent settlement.

930—Representative and democratic government was founded by pagan chiefs on the plain of Thingvellir. This was the organization of the Icelandic Commonwealth.

1000—Christianity was adopted by the law of Olaf Tryggvason, King of Norway. Leifur, son of Eirukur the Red, discovers "Wineland the Good," or North America.

1056—First school founded at Skalholt by Bishop Isleif Gissurarson.

1100—Son of Bishop Gissurarson, Teitur, founded a school at Haukadal.

A.D.

1107—Second school founded at Holar by Bishop Jon Ogmunds-son.

1133—Monastery of Thingeyri founded, oldest monastery in Iceland.

1178—Birth of Snorri Sturluson, famous Icelandic historian, at Reykholt.

1200—School at Holar closed due to lack of funds.

1236—Skalholt school closed.

1270—School at Holar re-founded.

1277—Church ordnance passed that all children 7 years of age should learn "Confession of Faith" and "Ave Maria."

1341—School at Holar closed again due to lack of funds.

1380—Iceland with Norway comes under Danish rule.

1393-1474—Nothing recorded concerning schools or teaching in Iceland.

1402—Black death sweeps the country.

1491—School at Skalholt refounded by Bishop Stefan Jonsson.

1530—Jon Arason, last Catholic Bishop in Iceland, set up the first printing, press.

1542—The Danish King, Christian III, passed the law that all children of Iceland should learn to read.   Also, two Latin Schools should be founded, one at Videy and one at Helgafell.   Neither was founded, due to lack of money. A children's school was to be founded at three monasteries in Skalholt Bishopric.   This was not carried out, due to lack of funds.

1552—First Grammar School founded at Holar.

1553—Bishops were ordered to maintain boarding schools for 24 pupils in each of the schools, Holar and Skalholt.

1571—Gudbrandur Thorlaksson becomes Bishop for Holar and publishes numerous books.   First Icelandic translation of the Bible.

1575—King Frederick II of Denmark issues decree that Deacons in monasteries of Holar Bishopric should teach children Luther's Short Catechism on Sundays.

1594—Luther's Short Catechism printed for the first time.

1610—Luther's Large Catechism printed in Iceland for the first time.

1635—Decree was issued by the King of Denmark that priests must visit homes and instruct the children.

1655—First Icelandic elementary reading book printed and used.

A.D.

1736—Jon Thorkelsson goes to Denmark to present school situation of Iceland to the King.

1741—Survey made of Icelandic schools by Ludwig Harboe, special emissary of King Christian VI of Denmark, and Jon Thorkelsson, former headmaster of the school at Skalholt.

1745—An elementary school was founded in Westmann Isles which lasted fifteen years.

1773—First Icelandic periodical published (monthly).

1784—Skalholt school destroyed in an earthquake. Most violent in history of Iceland.

1791—First permanent school founded at Hausastadir. It is still in existence.

1792—Library founded by Stefan Thorarensen, district leader or sheriff for Hunavatns, Skagafjardar and Eyjafjardarsysla.

1794—Library founded for the southern districts of Iceland by Rev. Markus Magnusson.

1799—Committee appointed to investigate school and church affairs in Iceland.

1801—Elementary school at Holar merged with elementary school in Reykjavik.

1804—Elementary school at Reykjavik was closed due to bad condition of the building.

1804–1805—No elementary schools in Iceland except the one at Hausastadir which had twelve pupils.

1810–1816—Great lack of elementary school books for the children.

1812—The school at Hausastadir closed, leaving no elementary school in Iceland.

1816—Icelandic Literary Society founded by the Dane, Rasmus Christian Rask.

1830—Private elementary school founded in Reykjavik with grants from the Thorkillis Fund.

1833—Reading Club founded at Flatey Island in Breifafjordur. This is the oldest reading club in the country.

1835—Periodical *Fjolnir* (personal name from the old Sagas), a cultural magazine published in Reykjavik.

1842—Jon Sigurdsson wrote an article on education in the periodical *Ny Fjelagsrit*, setting forth educational problems of the period.

1846—School at Bessastadir is moved to Reykjavik. This is the beginning of the Latin or Grammar School in Reykjavik.

A.D.

1847—Theological Seminary founded in Reykjavik. This was the beginning of the first faculty of the University.

1852—An elementary school founded at Stokkseyri.

1853—Proposed legislation regarding elementary schools in Iceland is discussed at the Althing.
Elementary reading book is published and distributed for the poor children.

1859—The Althing agrees to the suggestion of founding of elementary school in Reykjavik.

1862—Elementary school founded in Reykjavik by an act of the Althing.

1870—Elementary school established at Akureyri.

1872—Elementary schools are founded at Gerdir in Gardur and at Grunnastadir.

1874—Elementary school founded at Isafjordur. A school for girls (Secondary) founded in Reykjavik called the Household School.

1876—Medical Faculty established in Reykjavik.

1877—Elementary school founded at Modruvellir. The Flensborg School founded at Hafnarfjordur. This school gave general education; the graduate from this school could not enter the Grammar School or University.

1879—Secondary school for girls founded at Blondas.

1880—An Agricultural School is founded at Olafsdal by Torfi Bjarnason. Law passed by the Althing making it compulsory for schools to teach reading, writing, arithmetic and religion.

1882—Farmers' School at Holar founded by an act of the Althing.

1883—Farmers' School at Eidar founded.

1889—The Society of Icelandic Elementary School Teachers founded.

1890—A total of sixteen Reading Clubs founded in Iceland.

1892—A department for training teachers for elementary schools founded at the Flensborg School at Hafnarfjordur.

1897—The first periodical for children is published in Reykjavik by Briet Bjornhedunsdottir, the first lady member of the Althing.

1904—A technical school is founded in Reykjavik. School for Deaf Mutes founded in Reykjavik.

1905—Commercial school is founded at Hvitarbakki by Sigurd Thoralfsson.

1907—The Education Act passed by the Althing.

A.D.

1908—Jon Thorarinson becomes the first Director of Public
Education. Teachers' Training School for elementary
teachers founded in Reykjavik. A Law Faculty is established by the Althing.

1911—The University of Iceland founded by an act of the Althing.

1915—The Marine Engineers' School founded in Reykjavik by
an act of the Althing.

1918—The Co-operative Society for Farmers establishes a Commercial School.

1919—Act was passed concerning appointments and salaries of
teachers.

1921—The Union of Icelandic Elementary School Teachers
founded.

1924—The quarterly periodical for teachers, *Menntamal,* is
started.

1929—The Althing passes an act creating District Schools.

1930—Largest elementary school building in Iceland is put into
use in Reykjavik. Capacity of five thousand students.
Home for feeble-minded children at Solheimar in Grimsnes
opened.
The secondary school at Akureyri gets grammar school
privileges by act of the Althing.

1931—A School of Music is founded in Reykjavik. A district
school at Reykir in Hrutafjordur is established.

1933—A School for the Blind is started by Blindravinafelag
Islands (Society for the Friends of Blind People).

1936—The Althing passes a law concerning textbooks being
printed by the State. The Althing revised the Education
Act of 1907, making school attendance compulsory from
7 to 14 years of age.

1939—A State Horticulture School at Hveragerdir started.
Established by an act of the Althing in 1937.

1940—A Commercial University started in Reykjavik.
British Army of Occupation arrives.

1941—School terms are reduced from one to two months, due to
war conditions and occupation of buildings by the British
Army.
United States Army of Occupation arrives.

1942—Grants are made by the Good Templar Organization for
the making of moving pictures of Iceland to be shown in
the schools for educational purposes.
Visual education is being stressed in the schools.
Grant of $15,000 made to the Medical Faculty of the
University of Iceland by the Rockefeller Institute.

Introduction

The history of education in Iceland is rather imperfectly known and has not been recorded to any great extent in the past. It may be divided into the following periods:

930 TO 1580 (when the Home and Church were the basis of all learning).—At this time the Nordic tribes, around the Baltic and North Seas, who had sailed to Iceland, Greenland and America, were slowly being Christianized. These were Northmen, seamen and pirates. Later in this period Canute, a Northman, ruled not only England but also Norway and Denmark. Probably the most important thing during this period was the beginning of printing in the country. Like all the rest of the world, Iceland had its problems, and the Church problem was not the least important one. It was a struggle between the monarch and the Pope. The Church had accumulated property and money, but while working for temporal things, education declined. However, during this period Iceland did produce two great historians, Snorri Sturluson and Sturla Thordarson. Their works are living to-day.

1580 TO 1907.—This period sees the beginning of organized schools; schools that had been started earlier in Skalholt and Holar. The Danish King, Christian III, had already passed the law that all children should learn to read. His reason for this law was to promote Christianity in Iceland. By knowing how to read, the people could study the Bible. This was all a part of the King's plan for gaining a foothold against Catholicism. From 1741 to 1745 a survey was made of the educational conditions in Iceland. This survey was made of the educational conditions in Iceland. This survey was a result of Jon Thorkelsson's plea to the King in behalf of the schools.

In 1791 a school was started which is in existence to-day— Hausastadada School, a boarding school for children. By 1800 practically all people of Iceland could read and write. Lack of money was the thing which most retarded progress during this period, but rapid gains were made. All money came from Denmark, and the schools suffered accordingly. However, after this date, Iceland was given some independence and was permitted to levy taxes for the schools. Progressive education was taking form. This leads up to the most important date in all Icelandic educational history, the passage of the Education Act.

1907 TO THE PRESENT DAY.—The Education Act was passed by Parliament in 1907. This Act contained such things as: division of the country into school districts, creation of compulsory school attendance and a Director of Public Education. The people as a whole became more interested in education after such important steps were taken by the Government. Better buildings were erected, more attention was given to health of the public and the teachers began to receive more consideration. These and many other things could only be arrived at by the driving power and force of a free people and a democratic government. With such a firm foundation as the education of Iceland has, it remains now to liberalize some of its methods and ideas. This liberalization will come in the very near future. New methods of teaching are gradually coming to the front. Progressive teachers visit foreign countries, including America, to get new educational ideas and methods of teaching.

Due to the efforts of these men truly radical changes have been made during the past few years in the Icelandic educational system. The educational leaders are very much alert to all modern methods which will bring improvements and benefit the pupils. Their objective is to foster a much broader outlook and a more democratic generation.

Influence on Icelandic Education

The history of Icelandic education is not chiefly a history of the schools of the country. Only a few of those Icelanders who have a higher education owe it to Icelandic schools, and in the development of the majority of well-bred Icelanders, who are now grown, the school has taken only a small part.

How great is the rôle played by the school in the education of the Icelander? It must be comparatively small. There are several reasons, of which the following should be mentioned:

1. The schools of earlier centuries were schools for theologists, officials, and for erudition in the proper sense. They only concerned a minimal layer of the population. The rest were educated by their family or by friends, as "barnfostur," or the custom of offering a son to a friend, and to have the son accepted for the purpose of educating him was a mark of high esteem and friendship.

2. The common elementary school has been in existence only a very short time.

3. Schools are in session only a few months during the winter.

4. In the country only a few annual classes are held by the school system for children ten to thirteen years of age. These classes, in most places, meet only a few weeks each year.

5. The demands on the children, made by the teachers of elementary schools in town, are low. The disciplinary power of

the teacher is very restrained as the will of the child is widely respected.

6. Winter epidemics and bad weather cause irregularities in attendance at school.

In spite of all this the standard of education is not low. In some respects one might call it comparatively high. What is it then, besides the school, that educates the Icelander? In early childhood the education appears to be rather deficient in comparison with mid-European education. Mothers let their children have their will, and the children are usually a great trouble in the streets of the town, all of which the adult Icelanders undergo patiently. Organized plays and games are rare with younger children. Few institutions like a "kindergarten" are working, compared to the number of children at large. Accidents often occur to children. It is due only to the special temperament of the Icelanders that accidents are not more frequent. It appears as if the nation does not know what to do with children until they enter the working age, which takes place early in life.

In the first place it is necessity which educates them. It is given by the conditions of the country. One might consider and work out various elements and what they demand from the nation. A few of these conditions are the northerly position, the isolation, the climate, the light conditions, the mountainous character of the country, the soil, the volcanism, the flora and the fauna. The kind of work to be done is a consequence of these natural resources of the country.

Icelandic children begin work at a very early age. Their little working power counts in the economic life and is paid for. A farm, for instance, cannot exist without children. Country children have their regular duties, which result from the organic life and work on farms. Town children take part in this work in summer and are very much desired for this purpose. Seafaring, fishing and fish-manufacturing occupy a number of very young workers' time. Older scholars, the teachers and students, earn their living in summer by practical work. In many cases this period gives them the financial basis for their studies in winter and represents the only income of the whole year. For many young people, the farm where they come from is the financial base, therefore their working power belongs to that farm when it is needed. The change of seasons plays a larger rôle in Iceland than in industrial countries.

It would be interesting to work out the question of how the school education is influenced by this early work. Certainly the understanding of necessity is better than usual at the same age. The children see the relation between work, necessities and life.

Comradeship is created through the interchanging of professions and conditions of living. Many times the student and his professor work together. The young people learn to adapt themselves on roads, fishing trawlers or farms, and they also learn the natural hospitality of the people of Iceland.

The second important factor in Icelandic education is tradition, represented by the family and society. The school itself is greatly bound to tradition, but it is only one of the many outlets of tradition. The feeling and behaviour of the good Icelander usually coincides with tradition so completely that it is difficult to say whether this is a consequence of education or of hereditary qualities lying dormant; probably both.

What is the aim of Icelandic education from the point of view of tradition? It can be observed in the Icelanders where they are at their best. And to a certain extent, everywhere, when foreign influence has not changed them. One may also read it in the thousand-year-old literature, among which the poem "Havamal" gives the most concise expression. It is also to be observed in every Saga. The chief demands are: Not to show one's thoughts and feelings, race dignity, virtue and intelligence.

The third element in Icelandic education is foreign influence. This element will not willingly be recognized by the Icelanders. It is represented by foreigners working in Iceland, by the Icelanders who have lived abroad, by printed letters, books, newspapers and magazines.

Even the Icelandic elementary school is built up according to foreign patterns, especially after the Danish school. Denmark never made a great effort to solve the problems which the Icelandic youth will eventually have to solve.

As to the higher schools, various foreign patterns have worked together with Icelandic ideas and methods until the Icelanders will be of the opinion that they can do without the foreign patterns. The Icelanders who have a good specialist education have all, more or less, completed their education abroad.

Between these two elements, tradition and foreign influence, lies tension and the possibility for development. Necessity will decide what will be done about the future in general. The conflict is partly open and partly latent; resting under a thin cover. At the moment, the conditions of war are not normal and the Icelanders are under pressure. The attitude of the young Icelander is cramped and not natural. Tradition is strong in most of them, but they cannot fulfill tradition's claims, which are:

1. To fight for independence.
2. To be hospitable.
3. Not to show one's feelings and thoughts.

Icelandic Culture

One may understand Icelandic education and its way of working only when Icelandic ideas of culture are understood, and this understanding of their culture must go back to the Nordic culture.

Icelanders have a different standard for things considered cultural, a throwback to Nordic culture. From early times a difference between world cultures existed and could be seen by drawing a line between the north and south, this line cutting through the middle of Germany. One culture came up from the south, another culture came down from the north. On the north we have the Scandinavian countries and England. On the south we have the western civilization of Greece, Arabia and the Roman Empire. The northern conception of life and culture was mythical, while the southern conception took definite form and shape and was reproduced in song and art.

The education of Iceland of to-day is revolving about one main point; namely, the characteristics of Icelandic culture which set it apart from the cultures of other countries. The Nordic people's culture has come down to the Icelandic nation.

Considering this point, one would say that Icelandic culture was rather limited, due to its no thaving any art, music, or sculpturing. However, this is not true. The reason these things are not developed goes back to the Nordic concept of culture, nothing tangible, but always mythical, such as the worship of Odin as the supreme being, the absence of an empire and just agreements between the heads of families. In fact, one of the most outstanding things about Iceland never really existed, that is, the capitol, or Thingvellir, the hub of the nation, yet only a barren spot in the country.

The Icelandic people actually have no philosophy or logical thinking. Everything comes from and is based on the Sagas. However, Icelandic literature is very rich. Probably no other country has richer literature.

If the Icelandic schools do not have the things other nations' schools have, it is not because of the shallowness of the people, nor the backwardness of the country, but is due to the close relation to the Nordic culture which does not show in outward form or expression.

PART II

CHAPTER I

FROM 930 TO THE 16TH CENTURY

One does not have to associate very long with the Icelanders before an element in their mental make-up becomes evident: they are great lovers of freedom; freedom of speech and thought. They hate oppression of any kind. They have learned by bitter experience that national liberty is the cornerstone of true progress and prosperity. This element in their nature is a heritage from their forefathers, the first settlers who came from Norway. In 870 Harald Fairhair had made himself supreme in Norway and treated the landed proprietors oppressively. Many of them left the country and went to Iceland. In the course of sixty years all the habitable parts of the country along the coast were settled. In 930 a representative and democratic government was founded by the pagan chiefs on the plain of Thingvellir. The Icelandic Parliament or Althing is, therefore, the oldest one in the world. Christianity was adopted by law in 1000, and two schools and bishoprics, those of Holar and Skalholt, were established. The Latin language and the learning of the west, introduced by Christianity, were warmly received by the Icelanders, as poetry and history had already been cultivated here more than elsewhere in the Scandinavian countries.

Among the most important works in Icelandic literature is the collection of ancient heathen songs called the elder or poetic Edda. National historic and romantic works known by the name of Sagas are quite numerous. Many of these are masterpieces of prose style and are still read with delight by the people of Iceland, not in translation but in the original. The Icelandic language is the oldest of the Scandinavian group of tongues and is believed to exhibit the Norse language nearly as it was spoken at the date of colonisation of Iceland. On that account it is sometimes called Old Norse.

The Icelandic Sagas bear witness to the fact that reading and writing were cultivated in Iceland from an early date. In ancient times the pagan chiefs had their children educated in the arts of reading and writing as well as physical culture and carrying of arms. But their nature was quite different from what it is to-day. It was the accepted opinion in heathen times that children belonged to the parents; that they were a kind of property which the parents might do with as they pleased. The ancient legal code justified exposure of infants, but it was up to the father to decide. The reason for educating their children was not so much love of their children as to advance the dignity, reputation and power of the family.

With the adoption of Christianity a radical change took place in the attitude of the parents toward their children. Exposure of children gradually came to an end. Up to this time the Althing had been the only true school of the people. As Christianity became a potent factor in the mental and moral life of the nation a new cultural period began to assert itself. The right of a child to live was determined by something higher and nobler than the pleasure or whim of his parents. The idea that all children, rich and poor, had an equal right to education began to gain ground. The credit for proclaiming this new idea belongs to the first Icelandic bishops. As early as 1056 Bishop Isleif Gissurarson founded a theological school at Skalholt which had a great cultural influence upon the life of the nation. Bishop Gissurarson was the first educator in Iceland.

In the beginning of the new century (1100) other schools were established, one at Holar by Bishop Jon Ogmundsson, another at Haukadal by the Bishop's son, Teitur, and the third at Odda by Saemundur the Wise, to whom the poetic Edda is accredited. From these schools graduated many of the most outstanding men of the country, among them Snorri Sturluson, author of the younger, or prose Edda and *Heimskringla*, or the Histories of the Norse Kings.[1]

The monasteries at that time were also centres of education. The abbots themselves conducted schools assisted by well-educated and capable men. The teaching conducted at these schools was, of course, primarily based upon the Christian doctrines and dogmas and, as a result, they were undoubtedly of paramount importance in stimulating steadily growing Church worship. It is of interest to note that in the beginning of the 13th century there were 330 churches and 420 priests in the country; 220 churches and 280 priests in the Skalholt bishopric and but 110 churches and 140 priests in the Holar bishopric. It is estimated that more than 20 priests graduated from these schools each year. The primary aim of these schools was, however, not to turn out so many priests each year but to prepare the students for their walk in life. The teaching had to be in harmony with the life work for which the majority of the students prepared themselves. The subjects taught were: Latin (the students had to learn the Psalter or the Old Testament Book of Psalms in

[1] These books are available in English.

Latin), grammar, verse-making, chanting, and even writing sermons.

It is hardly possible to estimate to the full extent the value of the early schools upon the literary and cultural development of national life in general. This was, indeed, the most flourishing period in the history of Iceland, poetically and ecclesiastically. The period, too, when its intercourse with the world was greatest; when the Icelanders travelled extensively, not only to the Scandinavian countries, but to Germany, England, France, the Netherlands, Rome and Constantinople as well.

This period of progress and peace did not last. As the 12th century wore on, dark, ominous clouds gathered on the horizon. Foreign aggression now began to endanger the independence of the country. The chieftains, who had become politically important and who thought of nothing but their own interests, sacrificed the social order and safety of the country in ever-increasing domestic feuds. The nation was indeed a house divided. The Sturlung period, 1200 to 1262, is one of the saddest chapters in the history of Iceland. And during this period the Icelanders lost their most precious possession: their independence.

It must not be forgotten that during this period of civil war there lived the two most gifted writers of the country: Snorri Sturluson and Sturla Thordarson, son of Snorri's brother, Thord Sturluson, who wrote a great historical work known as the *Sturlungasaga* (the Saga of the Sturlung). But the great Snorri came to an untimely end. He was assassinated by the servants of the treacherous and malevolent Gizur Thorvaldsson, erstwhile son-in-law of Snorri, at his house in Reykholt, September 22, 1241, at the age of sixty-three.

It is asserted by some that general education during the commonwealth was better in Iceland than in other countries. But during the 13th and 14th centuries a drastic decline began. Despite the steadily increasing power of the church, the bishops and priests now thought more of furthering the temporal interests of the church than of educating the people. A fierce struggle ensued between the clergy and the farmers concerning the power and the privileges of the church. Although paganism was dead, never to return, and although a reign-of-law had been substituted for a reign-of-terror, the social life in Iceland during the 14th century was prone to relapse into the old channels of violence. Murders and other atrocities were still of frequent occurrence. There was turmoil in the monasteries and occasional violence. The people, during the Sturlung period, had been at the mercy of the rival chieftains; now they were at the mercy of the powerful Catholic Church. Their public spirit had been destroyed, and they had to wage their own hard battle for existence without any true guidance or leadership, temporal or spiritual. As a result public education came to an end. The schools fell into disuse. The school at Skalholt closed down in 1236; the one at Holar about 1200. The Holar School was refounded in the latter part of the 13th century, but fell into permanent disuse in 1341. From 1393 to 1474 there is hardly any mention of school teaching. The reasons for this are numerous. Many calamities befell the Icelandic people in the 14th century. Epidemics, famine and cattle diseases had sorely tried the people in the previous century; but a series of great misfortunes began with the eruption of Mount Hekla in 1300, accompanied by violent earthquakes which destroyed many farmsteads. The year following an epidemic broke out which carried away hundreds of people. Volcanic eruptions and destructive earthquakes were of frequent occurrence.

In the year 1339 an earthquake took place in southern Iceland destroying many farmsteads and killing many people. This was followed by a new eruption of Hekla in 1341 which had disastrous consequences. The meadows were buried under heavy deposits of ash which destroyed vegetation, causing the death of the farmers' livestock through shortage of grazing and fodder. Severe cattle diseases raged and many farmers lost all their earthly possessions. But that was not all, in the beginning of the 15th century the Black Death raged like wild-fire for three long years. People died by hundreds in deplorable helplessness. After the epidemic whole districts were devastated.

All these disasters and frequent misfortunes had a detrimental effect on the economic life of the country and on the mental life of the people. They had more vital things to thing about than schools and education. It is a marvel that the people could survive such recurring calamities. Although the old educational establishments had fallen into disuse, it is evident that those young people who were supposed to fill the vacant public offices received private instruction at the pastorages and monasteries.

As will be seen from the above, there were, up to the Reformation, many ups and downs in the educational history of Iceland. Despite great misfortunes, hunger and poverty, the spirit of the true pioneer still prevailed. The constant battle with adversity brought out the finest traits in their characters: courage and fortitude. People endowed with this noble spirit are bound to win in the end.

CHAPTER II

FROM 1538, THE REFORMATION, TO 1907, THE EDUCATION ACT

One important result of the Reformation in 1538 was renewed interest in education and in literary activity. It is stated that through the persuasion and advice of Bishop Gizur Einarsson, chief supporter of the Reformation, the King of Denmark, Christian III, issued a decree to the effect that schools should be founded in Iceland. Grammar schools (Latin Schools) on the island of Videy, a short distance from Reykjavik, and at Helgafell, and elementary schools in three monasteries in the Skalholt diocese. The royal officials opposed the decree, and as late as 1552 no schools had been founded. In that year Paul Huiffeldt came on a special mission to Iceland. He brought orders from the King that Latin Schools be maintained at both the bishops' seats, Skalholt and Holar. The school at Skalholt should have forty pupils and the one at Holar twenty-four. Bishop Gudbrandur Thorlaksson founded a grammar school at Holar the same year and Bishop Odd Einarsson at Skalholt a year later.

It is worthy of mention that Bishop Thorlaksson laboured with greater diligence and earnestness than anyone else in this period to make the Christian religion a driving force in the hearts and lives of his countrymen. He was interested in providing a proper reading matter for his people by translating the Holy Bible into Icelandic. It was printed at Holar in 1584. According to tradition the first printing press in Iceland was established at Holar by Bishop Jon Arason about 1530. Printing was an important factor in furthering the Reformation and bringing forth the spiritual life of the country.

The chief purpose of these newly established schools was to educate clergymen in reading, writing, singing, Latin, rhetoric, verse-making, theology, history, arithmetic, geometry, astronomy and calendar making. In the beginning of the 17th century Greek was included. At first the teachers were mostly Danish, but soon capable Icelandic teachers took their places. Before the Reformation the schools of Skalholt, Holar and Haukodalur were founded mostly on German culture because of the theological training gained in Germany. The Oddi School was based on French culture. After graduation from these schools the students were encouraged to go abroad and seek higher education at some foreign university, and as the Danish government gave free board and later free lodging to Icelandic students most of them went to the University of Copenhagen.

The introduction of the Lutheran doctrine had, undoubtedly, deep and lasting influence upon the mental and spiritual life of the people. The important literary achievements of that period bear witness to a new creative activity. The Icelanders were experiencing a literary renaissance which kindled new light and new hope in the hearts of a sorely tried people. Higher learning was cultivated with remarkable diligence, and in no land was the number of talented and well-educated men as large relatively as in Iceland. Due to the effort of those able men progress was made despite the fact that the King diverted to the royal treasury resources rightly belonging to the monasteries which should have been used for the building of schools for the people.

In the last part of the 17th century a new series of misfortunes and disasters befell the Icelandic people. Cold winters, volcanic eruptions and severe epidemics increased the difficulties under which the people were struggling. Overseas trade, upon whch the people depended, was at times completely interrupted by European conflicts. Owing to such calamities, famine and disease swept away the stricken people, and according to old annals, 1,100 people died from hunger and sickness in Thingey-jarthing and 1,400 in Mulathing from the middle of the year 1674 to 1675. In 1696 the winter was so severe that the ocean all around Iceland was ice-bound. In 1693 Hekla erupted so violently that ashes fell as far away as Scotland and Norway. But even worse than all this was the Danish trade monopoly which tended to deprive the common people of all hope of progress and economic well-being.

The beginning of the 18th century was no more promising. In 1707 a smallpox epidemic swept the country carrying away 18,000 people, or about one-third of the entire population. In 1727 there occurred an eruption of Oraefajokull which lasted from August 3rd to May 25th the following year. Hundreds of sheep and horses were killed and many farms were completely wiped out. In 1755 an eruption of Katla destroyed many farms and buried a large part of Skaftafellssysla under a deposit of ashes so deep that fifty farms had to be abandoned. A violent outbreak of Skatarjokull took place in 1783, one of the most destructive in the history of the country. Nine farms were blotted off the face of the earth, twenty-nine were ruined and two parishes were rendered uninhabitable for two years. The loss of animals amounted to 11,461 head of cattle, 190,448 sheep and 28,013 horses. As a result of this calamity it is estimated that more than 9,000 people died from hunger and attendant diseases. A distinguished Icelander, writing about Iceland in the 18th century states, "Iceland experienced forty-three years of distress due to cold winters, ice-floes, failures of fisheries, shipwrecks, volcanic eruptions, earthquakes, epidemics and contagious diseases among men and animals, which often came separately, but more often in connection with, and as a result of, one another."[1]

Such calamities are scarcely to be met with elsewhere in history. As can be readily imagined, the abject poverty and hopeless conditions of the Icelanders destroyed their optimism for the future and their spirit of progress and enterprise. The only thing they could even hope to accomplish was to keep themselves and their families alive.

When these days of trouble had passed, signs of national revival soon began to appear despite disheartening economic and social conditions. New and able men came upon the scene, inspired by noble ideals; Jon Vidalin, bishop at Skalholt, 1698 to 1720; Jon Arnason, bishop of Skalholt, former headmaster at Holar; and Jon Thorkelsson, headmaster at Skalholt, to mention only a few. These men did not spare any effort to promote public education in the country. Jon Thorkelsson was a young man when he became headmaster of the school at Skalholt. He was a man of firm character, but sensitive. He felt keenly the deplorable condition of the people and was passionately anxious to lift his countrymen to a higher level, morally and educationally. He had not been headmaster at Skalholt for many years when he could no longer endure the intolerable state of affairs in educational matters. He resigned from the school, went to Denmark in 1736 on his own accord and appealed to the King. That was by no means an easy mission. His appeal had, however, some result. A clergyman by the name of Ludwig Harboe, was sent by Christian VI on a special mission to Iceland to investigate matters. Jon Thorkelsson was his secretary and interpreter as he did not speak Icelandic.

As a result of profound suffering and unparalleled oppression from the Danish merchants, who had by lawless terror succeeded in gaining almost complete control over Icelandic trade for a time, the Icelanders were suspicious and even afraid of all Danish interference with their personal affairs. When they heard that Harboe was expected to be in Iceland soon they even imagined that his true purpose was to force them to accept heathen religion.

Harboe was a man of noble character, well-educated and just. He soon gained the confidence of the Icelanders and they paid him due respect. He travelled about the country, together with his secretary, in the years 1741 to 1745. The state of affairs was very discouraging. The nation as a whole was in a sad plight. The people were dispirited, due to all kinds of misery, oppression,

[1] Magnus Stephansen: *Island; i dat 18de Aarhundrede.*

superstition, hunger and poverty.   Their interest in schools was,
therefore, rather limited.   It was also quite hard to maintain
the two schools, due to financial difficulties and disagreement
between the Government and the officials.   Another thing which
increased the difficulties was the fact that the school buildings at
Skalholt had been destroyed in an earthquake in 1782.   The
bishops were anxious to get rid of the schools, due to diminishing
income.   After many long and serious discussions it was finally
decided to remove the school to Reykjavik, when the plan to
deport all the inhabitants of the country to Denmark came to
naught.   The school was not rebuilt until 1787.   In 1801 the
schools at Skalholt and Holar were united into one Latin School,
located at Reykjavik, which was a town of 300 inhabitants at
that time.   In 1804 the school house was in such bad condition
that it was deemed unfit for use.   A year later a grammar school
was established at Bessastadir.   This school is considered by
some to have been the best educational institution Iceland has
ever had.   Forty years later the school was again removed to
Reykjavik and has been there since.

Harboe and his associate, Jon Thorkelsson, suggested many
improvements in educational matters, some of which were immedi-
ately put into effect.   Harboe stressed the importance of instruct-
ing children in the Christian religion.   He had brought with him
a catechism, called Ponti, because it was written by Eirik
Pontoppidan, bishop of the Danish island of Sealand.   But in
order that the children derive full benefit from this book in
preparation for confirmation they had to be taught to read.
Confirmation had been prescribed by law in 1736, but had been
neglected since the death of Bishop Gudbrandur Thorlaksson,
1627.   Now a new ordinance was issued to the effect that the
priests should make house visitations three times a year and
attend to the education of children.   Parents in tolerable circumstances were compelled to hire literate, male or female, servants
to teach their children to read.   The result of these measures
was that in the 19th century nearly every adult person in Iceland
could read.

When Harboe and Thorkelsson had finished their investigation
they returned to Copenhagen.   Harboe became bishop of Sealand.
Jon Thorkelsson never returned to his native country.   Although
he did not live long enough to see his greatest hopes materialize,
it cannot be said that his was labour lost.   He died in 1759
without ever receiving any token of appreciation from his people
whom he had truly loved to the end of his days.   He remained
true to his ideals, his people and his country.   In his last will he
gave all his possessions—books, money and estates—to the poor

Place of Execution of Jon Arason

orphan children in the district of Kjalarnes. A nobler gift has never been given to the children of Iceland. Jon Thorkelsson was indeed a man with the spirit of a true reformer. His magnificent courage and effort reflect his character and dignity.

As previously stated, the Lutheran Reformation inspired some literary activity in Iceland. It was brought to the country when national life was at a low ebb. The Catholic Church had been true to the Roman hierarchy, but neglected the spirit of true Christianity. Many of the bishops had been inefficient old men, foreign adventurers, or ruthless favourites of kings, who were interested only in their own selves. The old literary activity had ceased as early as 1400. Little attention, possibly none, was given to learning. The people were even forbidden to read the Icelandic Sagas. There was retrogression and decay in every sphere. Reaction was bound to set in and it did appear. It came in the form of the Lutheran Reformation and it spelled the downfall of the Catholic hierarchy in Iceland. This struggle amounted to physical force in many instances between the King's men and the bishops and their supporters. The ultimate result was the execution of the last Catholic bishop, Jon Arason, and his two sons at Skalholt on November 7, 1550.

The period 1550 to 1745 saw the country gradually regaining its feet after being beaten to its knees by the struggle of the Reformation. The people's attention was diverted from religion to practical and more general problems and to education.

The first elementary school in Iceland was founded in the Westmann Isles in the year 1745. This school had a short history. It was discontinued 15 years after its founding. The next elementary school was established at Hausastadir in Alftanes in 1791, with a grant from the Thorkillis (Thorkelsson) Fund. It was a boarding school attended by 12 to 16 children. This school ceased to exist in 1812.

The 18th century had passed. It had been a period of great calamities for the Icelandic nation. The new century gave new hope. There was a dawn of a new day in the mental and spiritual life of the people. It was not, however, until 1830 that an elementary school was founded in Reykjavik, which had at that time about 500 inhabitants and 70 to 80 children. The time was ripe for new, constructive ideas. A new pioneer comes upon the scene, Jon Sigurdsson, the most beloved leader of the Icelandic nation.

CHAPTER III

JON SIGURDSSON

Of the outstanding names in the history of Iceland the name of Jon Sigurdsson stands out in bold relief. He is the true liberator of the country and his name will shine in the history of Iceland for ages to come. This great man was born at Hrafnseyri in the north-western part of Iceland, on June 17, 1811. He spent many years of his life in Denmark and resided in Copenhagen after entering the university there.

He was a man of great talent who devoted himself to history, archaeology and philology. His scholarly activity attracted great attention among the educated class. He published the first volume of the Icelandic Sagas for the Royal Northern Text Society, the "Younger Edda," and he also wrote a catalogue of Icelandic manuscripts in Copenhagen, Stockholm and Uppsala in Norway. Furthermore, he published the first volume of the *Diplomatarium Islandicum*, and assisted in the publication of other great works, such as *Regista Diplomatica Historia Danicae*. He wrote numerous articles on philology. He became secretary of the Arnemagnean Commission in 1848, and held this position until his death.

Although he distinguished himself as a great scholar, it was in the field of practical politics that he won lasting renown. He became a self-chosen leader of the Icelanders in their hard struggle for national liberty and independence. As early as 1832 Jon Sigurdsson began a stormy agitation for improvement of the school system. He suggested that public schools for children be erected where they were easy to reach, and that agricultural schools be founded in all parts of the country. He also proposed that a theological school be established in the capitol and that the Latin School be moved from Bessastadir to Reykjavik and its courses improved. He proposed further that instruction should be given in jurisprudence and medicine.

Such an extensive educational programme could not be carried out, due to economic reasons, but the work was undertaken gradually. In 1846 the Latin School was moved to Reykjavik and a theological seminary was established the following year. The plan to establish a medical school in Reykjavik had to be postponed despite the fact that epidemics were of frequent occurrence and there were only six or seven trained physicians in the country. The Danish Government also opposed the attempt to found a law school in Iceland. The Danish Government considered Iceland as a province and ruled it accordingly.

Grammar School in Reykjavik

As a result, Icelandic law students were taught to look upon all questions from the Danish point of view and became enthusiastic supporters of the Danish Crown. This acted, of course, as a brake on patriotic sentiment in Iceland. As this is not the proper place to describe the events influencing the political thoughts in Europe since the French Revolution, no attempt will be made to do so. New national spirit and liberal sentiment began to present themselves all over the world. After the July revolution in France, in 1830, and the downfall of Napoleon Bonaparte, the European monarchs hastened to revise their policies in order to save their own skins.

In Iceland this new spirit of liberty began to find an echo in the hearts of the Icelandic poets. In 1835 the periodical *Fjolnir* was founded in Copenhagen by Thomas Saemundsson; the poet, Jonas Hallgrimsson; the philologist, Konrad Gislason; and the jurist, Brynjalf Petursson. The purposes of this periodical were to stimulate patriotism and love of liberty, purify the Icelandic language and reform Icelandic literature. The effect of this undertaking on the slumbering Icelandic spirit was tremendous. The names of these men will never fade from the pages of Icelandic history.

In 1831 King Frederick VI deemed it advisable to pay some heed to growing public sentiment, and with the aid of liberal-minded statesmen, assemblies of estates were organized which were to serve as advisory bodies to the King. Iceland was not to be forgotten. It was to be represented by two delegates elected by the people. This could by no means satisfy the patriotic aspirations of the Icelanders. A petition for a separate assembly was sent to Denmark which had as its effect the formation of a commission of ten royal officials in 1838. This arrangement proved to be unsatisfactory to the Icelanders. But in 1840 King Christian VIII, who ascended the throne in 1839, suggested to the commission the advisability of establishing a national assembly, or Althing, with representatives chosen by the Icelandic people. The dawn of national liberty had finally appeared upon the horizon.

There was great rejoicing in Iceland when the Althing was re-established March 8, 1843. But even if this was an important step in the right direction, there were many serious defects in the fundamental law for Iceland as sanctioned by the King. Only owners of definite amounts of land had the right to vote. The representatives were to be only twenty, chosen by the people against six appointed by the King. Those of the representatives who could not speak the Icelandic language were permitted to use the Danish language at the deliberations of the Althing, their speech being translated by the presiding officer. Demands for important changes were brought forward, but as they were considered too radical they found little support.

This was the state of affairs when Jon Sigurdsson came into the picture. He had already, in 1841, started and edited the publication of a periodical called *Ny felagsrit*. In this organ the important problem of education, trade, finance and politics were discussed with frankness and farsightedness. In the first volumes of this periodical he outlined the programme of independent national legislature for the Icelandic nation. And as soon as the Althing had been established in 1843 he demanded complete abolition of the Danish trade monopoly, under which the Icelandic people had suffered for centuries.

Jon Sigurdsson was a man of great discernment and clear judgment. He had all the qualifications of a great leader and he felt keenly the sad plight of his people. There were, to his mind, three questions of vital importance that needed speedy solution: self-government for the people, general education and free trade.

He stated that the progress of the people depended mainly upon the solution of these questions. "The Althing," he said, "will awaken the national life and the national spirit; the school will kindle the spiritual life and the spiritual power and furnish all the knowledge which will make men fit to accomplish all the good possible; and the trade will substantially strengthen the national power, create national prosperity, increase and improve the industry and the trades, and, consequently, stimulate further the spiritual so that it will become a new foundation for progress and prosperity as time goes on."[1]   He then discussed the necessity of establishing schools for all classes of people, the common, the middle and the upper class. He said, "In Iceland there are mostly two classes of people; the common people and the educated class. The middle class is practically non-existent. It is, therefore, necessary to create this class as soon as possible, but it is even more important to promote the education of the farmer class of our country, and we are more capable of doing this than many other countries."

"The purpose of the school as regards the people wil be to prepare each class so that it will be able, in its respective field, to aid the progress of the country, of the nation as a whole, in order that we may gradually develop to such an extent as to be able to keep abreast of the progress of the civilized nations during each century, as conditions may permit, and to overcome all obstacles in our path, but whether we succeed or not the Althing will best demonstrate.   To reach this goal we should all do our

---

[1] From *Ny felagsrit* (Vol. II, 1842).

share with diligence and care and not shrink from any additional expense we can possibly bear, because no money is better spent than that for which is bought spiritual and substantial progress within reach. Let us elevate our thoughts and demonstrate our energy and hereditary strength which we have received from our distinguished forefathers, by overcoming all obstacles which can be overcome with the power of money and knowledge. If we make it our rule never to elevate our thoughts then we will soon come to the point where we look upon everything with timidity, despondency and apprehension."[1]

Such was the spirit of his message to the people who had known nothing for ages but oppression, misery and suffering. It was an appeal to their higher sentiments, which sentiments had been neglected and despised by the rulers and their officials.

But in order that the reader may obtain some idea of the conditions prevailing among the Icelandic people at this period, due to the Danish trade monopoly, mention will be made of a few facts which will illustrate what Jon Sigurdsson and his followers, as well as the people themselves, had to fight against.

King Frederick III had inaugurated the policy, which his successors followed conscientiously, that no "foreigners," except the Danes themselves, should be permitted to trade with the Icelanders, and any one who dared to violate these regulations, even if he did so only in extreme need, had to face severe punishment. It often happened during this period that English and Dutch fishing vessels traded secretly with the Icelanders, who were tempted to take the risk, especially when the Danish merchants refused to buy their goods. In 1678 a man, Pall Torfason by name, a district chief in Isafjord on the western coast of Iceland, had broken the trade regulations by buying a couple of fishing lines from an English fishing boat in exchange for a few articles of knitted goods which the Danish merchants had refused to buy. Pall was brought to trial for violating the regulations. He was found guilty, and as a punishment he suffered the loss of all his household articles despite the fact that he could prove beyond doubt that without the fishing lines he could not have continued fishing.[2] Trading outside one's district was also punished with the same severity. Six years later the price on imported goods was increased, but the price on Icelandic articles of export was lowered proportionally. At the same time punishment for violation of trade regulations was made still more severe. Trading with foreigners or outside one's district was punished

---

[1] From *Ny felagsrit* (Vol. II, 1842).

[2] *Saga Islendinga Seytjanda Old* (The History of Iceland in the 17th Century), by Pall Eggert Olasson.

by flogging, loss of property or imprisonment for years in the fortress of Bremerholm, the Danish "Devil's Island" of that period. In 1699 a poor peasant was flogged in the presence of the Danish district magistrate for selling a few fish outside his district because the Danish merchants in his district would not buy them. These are not isolated instances. In 1700 two men were sentenced to imprisonment in the fortress of Bremerholm, and the loss of all their household goods, for buying a few yards of kersey from an English fisherman.[1]

The people of Iceland were completely at the mercy of the Danish merchants and their protectors, the district magistrates, who received their share in the profit of this racket. The Danish merchants were under no legal obligation whatsoever to buy Icelandic goods, and in many instances when the people from the interior of the country finally after a difficult and trying journey reached the seaport with their goods, the merchants either flatly refused to buy their articles, or just bought a limited amount. To bring the goods back home required so much labour and expense that many preferred to abandon them at the local port and go home to their families disappointed and empty-handed.

Often large quantities of fish, meat and hides and hundreds of barrels of train-oil had to be destroyed as the merchants refused to buy these articles. It must have been a heart-rending experience for these poor and oppressed people to see their goods, which they had slaved to produce, destroyed before their eyes. Such merciless treatment at the hands of their oppressors, the Danish merchants, could only result in despondency and destruction of all spirit of enterprise, which is of paramount importance to the growth of national life. This was also bound to ruin the morals of the people, and it seems that Danish merchants who were shrewd businessmen, even according to modern standards, did not fail to take advantage of the situation. Frequently they bought Icelandic goods for high-priced brandy which only served to increase the misery of the people. This was not the only time in the history of man when representatives of civilized countries have tried to destroy the spirit of independent national life with oppression and "fire-water."

When the voice of Jon Sigurdsson echoed throughout the land the Danish trade regulations were still in effect. After the reestablishment of the Althing (1843) Jon Sigurdsson and his supporters began a new agitation for the abolition of those "hangman's regulations," the Danish trade monopoly. The Danish merchants tried to thwart the movement. A petition

---

[1] *Saga Islendinga Seytjanda Old* (The History of Iceland in the 17th Century), by Pall Eggert Olasson.

was sent to Denmark, and strangely enough it found numerous supporters among the members of the Danish Sigsdag (Parliament). Ten years elapsed, years of "attack and counter-attack," and finally, on April 15, 1854, the bill for abolition of the trade monopoly became law. The fetters on free trade which had weighed heavily upon the Icelanders for two hundred and fifty years were finally broken. The first stronghold obstructing the road to national liberty had fallen. It was an important victory in the struggle for the "Rights of Man."

It is not possible to give a detailed account of the life and work of Jon Sigurdsson in a book of this character. This great leader had the good fortune to see some of his most cherished hopes materialize. On June 5, 1874, King Christian IX granted self-government and legislative power to Iceland. The governor, or "Landshofding," as he was called by the Icelanders, had executive power in domestic affairs. He was, however, not responsible to the Althing but to the Minister for Icelandic affairs in Denmark. In this year (1874) there occurred the millennial anniversary of the settlement of Iceland. The constitution, granted by the King, became effective August 1, 1874. The millennial anniversary of the country and the inauguration of the new government were celebrated with as much gusto as the population could give occasion to. The King of Denmark, Christian IX, visited the country and was received with enthusiasm. Delegates from foreign countries, Norway, Sweden, France, Germany and the United States, were present at the celebration. The American poet, Bayard Taylor, spoke on this occasion for the United States, and in his book *Egypt and Iceland* he gives a vivid description of this great event.

A new pinnacle had been reached on the toilsome road to complete liberty and independence. The spirit behind these accomplishments was that of Jon Sigurdsson, who laboured relentlessly for the liberation of the country and for the complete overthrow of Danish rule in Iceland. He had succeeded in awakening the national consciousness and had made the people elevate their thoughts to higher and nobler aims in life than just to live. He had won recognition for his people as a distinct unit in the confederation of nations.

The economic condition of the country improved gradually after the abolition of the trade restrictions. A new spirit of enterprise began to manifest itself and there began a period of intellectual activity which has never ceased. Schools were founded all over the country. A medical school was founded in Reykjavik in 1876 to take care of the steadily-growing demand for trained physicians. A new age of learning was dawning for the Icelandic people which culminated in the establishment of the University of Iceland in 1911. It was dedicated on the birthday of Jon Sigurdsson, June 17, with fitting ceremonies.

Although the Icelanders had received their constitution Jon Sigurdsson was not satisfied. He regarded this as only a land-mark on the road to complete independence of the Icelandic nation. That was his sublime goal. But he did not live long enough to see his vision come true. He died in 1879 and was buried in the old cemetery in Reykjavik with great solemnity. He had resigned his life, but his spirit still lives. His birthday is a national holiday, and on this day each year a wreath is placed upon his grave in the name of the people.

"To live in the soul of the people is not to die."

CHAPTER IV

1907 TO 1941

Far-reaching improvements in school affairs were not forth-coming until 1874, when Iceland received its constitution and entered upon a new era of national development. In 1880 a bill was passed by the Althing regarding the teaching of reading, writing and arithmetic in the public schools, which were few in number at that time. After 1880 rapid progress was made in educational affairs. During the year 1887 and 1888 it is estimated that about 46 children had attended schools in the country and 30 elementary schools had been in activity during that year. The subjects taught in these schools were reading, writing, arithmetic, spelling, geography, catechism and Bible history. The school period was from 5 to 7 months.

The greatest step in public education was made in 1907 when the Althing passed the Education Act which made school attend-ance compulsory from 7 to 14 years of age. From that time general interest in public education began to assert itself, especially among the clergymen. The sponsor of this act was Jon Thorarins-son, member of the Althing at that time, and later the first director of public education in Iceland. From then on the progress of public education has been steady and rapid.

In 1918 the Althing passed an Entertainment Tax Law which collects 20 per cent. on entertainment admissions. In 1927 this law was amended to give all proceeds of this tax to a fund for building a National Theatre in Reykjavik.

This law sets forth the following: In cities 1,500 and over entertainment tax prevails. Taxable entertainments are con-certs and musical entertainments, theatricals, lectures and

Elementary School in Reykjavik

Note how the building is built so as to provide a windbreak

recitals, moving pictures and slides and tumbling acts, with a 10 per cent. tax added to each admission. Dances, private and public, if held until after 11 p.m., sleight-of-hand acts, variety shows and other public entertainments where admissions are charged and which were not mentioned before are taxed 20 per cent. on each admission. Owners of billiard halls pay 30 kronur ($4.50)[1] per month per table. Tables are security.

Exemptions are as follows: Inexpensive educational lectures, entertainments supporting charities, entertainments for members or guests of a society and school dances other than those of regular dancing schools.

The tax is to form a separate fund called "National Theatre Fund." The fund is to be applied to building a national theatre in Reykjavik and to support theatricals produced in this theatre.

The board of governors, three, will manage the fund. They are appointed by the Ministry of Education; they receive no pay. This board invests the fund and prepares for the creation of the building under the supervision of the Ministry of Education. The State is to supply a free building lot. Violations of this law bring a fine of from 50 to 500 kronur ($7.50 to $75.00).

In 1919 an act was passed by the Althing which set forth the methods by which teachers should be appointed to their teaching positions in elementary schools and how their salaries would be paid. This act was the first regulation of teachers in Iceland. The law stated the following:

1. To be appointed a teacher in an elementary school supported by public funds the applicant must be:

(a) Free of any conviction of a misdemeanor and have good morals.

(b) Be a graduate of a teacher training school or grammar school.

(c) Have had a course in the science of teaching and child development, or have been a teacher for three years with a letter of recommendation from a clergyman or the last school board for which he worked.

(d) Have a certificate showing good health.

(e) Be at least 21 years of age.

2. If a vacancy exists in a school, the school advertises in the official government paper and teachers' periodicals. They must advertise the vacancy for two months. After the applications have been received the school board meets and selects its choice of a teacher and submits his name to the Director of

---

[1] Throughout this paper the chan ge from kronur to dollar is only approximate, uniformly changed at 15c. per kronur.

Public Education who will appoint or reject the applicant. The school board must have a copy of the applicant's qualifications and certificates, and recommendations from the last job if having taught before.

3. If none of the applicants have teachers' certificates or are graduates of a grammar school the board must obtain an able man or woman to teach the school until such time as a qualified teacher may be selected.

4. A teacher's appointment and salary begin at the beginning of the school term.

5. If a teacher resigns he must announce his resignation to the school board in advance.

6. All teachers in daily behaviour must be a model of conduct and do their duty with utmost care.

7. If a teacher is not satisfactory the school board may dismiss him with notice, and in extreme cases without notice.

8. The salaries of teachers shall be decided and regulated by the Althing.

9. If by law a school district is altered and a teacher is not needed, he has no claim for reimbursement after he has had notice of termination of his services.

In 1926 the Althing revised, amended and added to the original Education Act of 1907. Under this revision compulsory school attendance began at 10 years of age and the teaching of religion was expanded. The following things were set forth in this Act of 1926:

1. The life and teaching of Christ were to be taught in the schools.

2. Fractions and decimals were added to the arithmetic course.

3. New courses in natural science and physiology were added to the school courses.

4. Drawing was to be taught in the elementary schools.

5. Movable or travelling schools were started in rural areas where no other schools were available. Children 10 to 14 years of age must attend not less than 12 weeks of school each year. If children get sufficient training at hoome as determined by the educational authorities and school board, the movable schools will not be necessary.

6. The local school boards may grant exceptions to school attendance if such pupils can pass the examinations in the spring of each school year.

7. The school boards may allow children less than 10 years of age to attend school, but never less than 7 years of age.

8. The location of all new schools will be determined by the Ministry of Education as well as specifications and plans for new buildings.

9. A yearly examination in those districts with no school will be given by a person appointed by the Director of Public Education.

10. All children from 8 to 14 years of age must attend the examinations in the spring. Those not attending will be examined at home and the parents will bear all necessary costs of this examination.

In 1936 the Althing revised this Act again, this time showing more modification and advancement. The main points of this revision were:

1. Compulsory school attendance shall start at 7 years of age.

2. Districts can make exceptions on school attendance. The child can postpone beginning school if the home training is adequate. The school board can grant these exceptions.

3. At 10 years of age the child must be able to read Icelandic, write all letters and easy words, do orally simple sums and solve everyday problems.

4. The child must have studied Iceland's outstanding men and know the history of the country.

5. He must know the chief industries of the larger countries of Europe, know the hemispheres and know the earth's place in the solar system.

6. Handiwork shall be taught in the elementary schools.

7. Gymnastics will be given with or without equipment.

8. In every school district a school house will be built in a location where all children may go home each day. If this is not possible, due to long distances, a boarding school shall be maintained. The cost of the child's board will be borne by the parents.

9. (a) The school term shall be 33 weeks per year at schools with 3 teachers and for children 7 to 9 years of age, or 500 hours' instruction during the year.

(b) In schools with 1 or 2 teachers and children 10 to 14 years of age the term will be 24 weeks, or 700 hours' instruction.

(c) 1 or 2 teacher schools with pupils 7 to 9 years of age, 24 weeks of instruction, or 700 hours.

In boarding schools each child has to stay 12 to 13 weeks per year, and between the ages of 7 to 14 years the child must attend school a total of 88 weeks.   Each child between 10 and 14 years of age must attend school at least 14 weeks per year.

10.   In each educational district a board of five members will have jurisdiction over all school matters.   In each district of the educational district a board of three members will be subordinate to the board of five and supervise all educational matters of their district.

11.   No foreign language is to be given except to those children who read and write their native tongue well and have a good knowledge of Icelandic grammar.

12.   The State pays the salary of the housekeeper of the boarding schools.   This salary to be decided by the Educational Director of Public Elementary Education.

13.   Each county and city of the country is to be an educational district.   Each educational district will have one or more school districts, each to have an elementary school.

14.   The headmaster of the school must be present at all school board meetings.   He has no vote but can make recommendations.

15.   When more than one person applies for a teaching position the board must make a first, second and third choice and forward to the Director of Public Education.   The board must have the advice of the headmaster on new appointments; however, the headmaster has no vote.   If the headmaster is to be hired, the board must seek the advice of an educational supervisor.

16.   Teachers of special subjects and substitute teachers are appointed by the headmaster with the consent of the school board and are paid only for the time spent in teaching.

17.   All school board reports are forwarded to the Educational Board.   In rural districts one of the board members is to be custodian of the funds.   He renders a report to the school board at the end of each year.

18.   The Director of Public Education issues a copy of school regulations to the various school districts who in turn use them as a base for their individual school regulations.

19.   In each district, educational, the county officials can establish a fund for the use of the schools.   Estimates are made by the school boards as to amounts needed for the year.   There can be donations of money or free labour for new buildings.

20.   The teachers in private schools must have the same qualifications as those in public schools.

21. *Examinations.* Every spring, children 8 to 14 years of age take an examination. Censors must be present at final examinations to give the marks. The censors are appointed by the school board. Their fee is the same as special teacher's pay. Final examinations are to be at the end of the term and never before April 1st. Absentees are compelled to take examinations, and if they fail to do so fines are imposed by the sheriff. If the child is 14 and deficient in some subject the school board, with the aid of the headmaster, must give special aid until the pupil passes the subjects in which he is deficient. The headmaster and a physician decide what the child's capabilities are.

22. *Supervisors.* They are to be appointed when the Althing votes the funds. The best teachers of the country are to be appointed to be supervisors. The country will be divided into districts with a supervisor in each. The duties of the supervisors will be set forth by the Director of Education.

23. The vacations in elementary schools will be as follows:

(*a*) December 1.

(*b*) Christmas—December 16 to January 3.

(*c*) Ash Wednesday.

(*d*) Easter—Palm Sunday to the third day after Easter Sunday.

(*e*) The first day of Summer (April).

(*f*) White Sunday (Whitsun), Saturday to Tuesday.

24. *Temporary rules.* When the Althing grants funds research will be started on the problems as to what is the best way to divide the country into school districts.

For each 50 children, 7 to 14 years of age, or 40 children, 10 to 14 years of age, in the day schools one teacher is to be added to the staff; 40 children, 10 to 14 years of age, at boarding schools one teacher is to be added.

At boarding schools headmasters and teachers are on probation for three years before being given a permanent contract.

In the revision of the Education Act of 1907 made in 1926 the duties of school boards of elementary schools were set forth.

The educational authorities supervise all examinations and keep all papers. If any student is deficient in his education the local school board is responsible for correcting this deficiency, such as getting special teachers to give training in the subjects in which the pupil is deficient. The parents pay the extra cost.

Each school board serves three years and may be re-elected. The chairman of the board calls the meetings as often as needed. Minutes of all meetings are recorded. The majority rules in all voting.

The school board sees that students' books are available, supervises teachers in general and sees that students are properly instructed. It submits a budget each year and supervises the spending of money. It makes all rules and regulations of the school and forwards to the Director of Public Education for approval. All accounts of the board are audited by the Municipal Directors where the school is located.

The health of teachers and students is supervised by the medical authorities of the State.

In 1937 the Teachers' Appointment Act of 1919 was amended. This new amendment indicates the growing strength of the teachers' organization of the country. The Teachers' Training School, by the Act of the Althing, now had the full responsibility of training the teachers and establishing the standards of this training.

1.   Conditions to gain an appointment as a teacher in the Icelandic schools under the new amendment were as follows:

(a) Never to have been found guilty of a misdemeanor.

(b) Have a diploma from the Teachers' Training School or be a graduate of the Grammar School. The Grammar School graduates must attend the Teachers' Training School for one year. They must take the course, "Methods of Teaching," and pass an examination in it. People who, in the opinion of the Educational Authorities, have special knowledge not in the curriculum of the Teachers' Training School, must attend the school one year anyway in the "Methods of Teaching" and pass an examination.

2.   The same rules apply to anyone founding or teaching in a private school. Educational authorities may grant exceptions upon sound recommendations.

3.   If applicants applying for jobs do not fulfil the requirements, the school board must get a teacher fulfilling the requirements as nearly as possible. School boards and headmasters of private schools report to the educational authorities each year as to what special teachers are to offer as well as the ones regularly appointed. They must include in this report that all such teachers are fulfilling their duties.

4.   This law does not apply to those teachers in the country who are already teaching, or have been teaching for some time. It applies to all new teachers just entering the profession.

In 1937 the Althing passed a law establishing a Travelling Book Library and an Educational Film Library.

The provisions of this law are as follows:

1. According to this law, book clubs outside of towns and villages with public library facilities are to be participants in grants as well as a library of educational films which is to be established under the supervision of the educational authorities.

2. The entertainment tax is to be increased by 15 per cent. from January 1, 1938, two-thirds of which is to form a fund for the aid of book clubs under the supervision of the educational adviser and one-third to establish a collection of educational films.

3. The book clubs are to send to the educational advisers each year their accounts and list of members if they desire to get financial aid from the fund. The book clubs have also to report how many books have been lent out during the year and to how many members. A list of books owned by the club is also to be furnished.

4. Financial aid is granted only on the receipt of a declaration of the Municipal Council that they are granting an amount equal to the National Fund grant to the book club.

5. The educational adviser allocates the grants in March for the following year.

6. The amount of the grant to be in proportion to the dues paid by members of the club during the year and never to exceed two kronur (30 cents) per member. The first allocation from the fund to take place in 1939.

7. Book clubs which have not sent in their accounts and applications before March 1 have no claim for financial aid from the National Fund.

8. Book clubs of good standing are, according to this law, to receive a free copy of *Hemsard* (Parliamentary Proceedings), Report of the Statistical Bureau Lawbook, Judgments of the Supreme Court of Iceland, Reports of the State Owned Schools, the Gazette, Reports of Parliamentary Committees, and other reports issued by public institutions. The publishers are to send the reports directly to the clubs.

9. No aid is to be given to any book club with less than ten members. The educational adviser is allowed to stop aiding irregularly conducted clubs until such irregularities have been corrected.

10. The Ministry of Education will issue by-laws, rules and regulations for these book clubs and the educational film library.

11. The collection of educational film is to be the property of the State. By-laws are to be issued as to the management, use and rental of the film and as to what schools and institutions are to have the privilege of using them.

In 1940 the Althing put into effect some new regulations con.cerning the Elementary School of Reykjavik. These regulations were as follows:

1. Object of the schools:

(a) To teach the pupils courtesy and to instil in them good habits of thought and behaviour.

(b) To give them a sound body and good health.

(c) To give them instructions according to the laws of the land.

2. All children 7 to 14 years of age are required by law to attend school.

3. The school physician may exempt a child from school attendance. The headmaster, the school board and the parents must see that mentally weak children get proper instruction.

4. The instruction in the school each day shall be according to the headmaster's schedule.

5. Vacations are set forth as follows:

(a) December 1.

(b) Christmas Vacation, December 20 to January 7.

(c) Ash Wednesday.

(d) Palm Sunday to the 3rd day after Easter Sunday.

(e) 1st day of Summer.

(f) Whitsun.

(g) Summer Vacation—June 16 to August 31.

(h) The headmaster is empowered to grant a free day each month.

6. The Minister of Education appoints the regular teachers in the Elementary Schools of Reykjavik and determines their duties. The headmaster selects the substitute teachers in consultation with the school board. Other personnel is selected by the Municipal Authorities.

7. The school board supervises the school through the headmaster.

8. The children are to be in the open between class periods if weather permits. If any child damages school property the parents are responsible for payment of damages.

9. Children must be equipped with all necessary books.

10. Those with any contagious disease will not attend school.

11. Any child violating any rules and orders of the school may be dismissed by the headmaster not to exceed two weeks. The school board decides on permanent dismissal of any students.

12. All children after they have passed their eighth birthday are required to take the annual examination. Only sickness will be an exemption.

13. If any child fails to pass the examinations in Icelandic, arithmetic, or writing, he must take the same subjects the following year.

14. Upon successful completion of the school the pupil receives a certificate which must be signed by the headmaster and the censors of the final examination.

15. The school must keep a record of attendance as well as all examination marks.

16. The records and reports are in the keeping of the headmaster.

17. Each year the headmaster will submit reports to the Educational Authorities.

18. The following subjects are to be taught in the Reykjavik Elementary Schools:

(a) Icelandic (reading, writing and grammar).

(b) Handwriting.

(c) Arithmetic.

(d) Public behaviour and customs of the native land.

(e) Religion.

(f) History, geography and natural history.

(g) Music (singing).

(h) Drawing.

(i) Handicraft.

(j) Gymnastics.

(k) Swimming.

(l) Preparation of meals (girls only).

In addition, foreign languages (Danish and English) will be given to those students who are proficient in their native tongue.

19. Schedules, subjects and examinations are to be in accordance with rules issued by the Educational Authorities.

20. The sanitation of schools and the health of the children are to be in accordance with regulations issued by the Ministry of Health.

In 1941 the Althing revised the regulations concerning elementary school textbooks.

1. The Minister of Education issues a list of books necessary for the fulfilment of the law of elementary education. The educators and the Director of Elementary Education advise as to the content and form of the books.

2. Whenever a school book is needed the publishers advise the Director of Elementary Education of such need. The publishers must keep abreast of changes. If no information has been received as to changes or alterations of the former book the same may be published again.

3. If the chairman of the school board deems it necessary to issue a new book in any of the branches it has to send in its recommendations as to the content and form of such book.

4. If two or more books are needed or recommended in the same branch the State Publishers have to issue such books as soon as possible.

5. The State Publishers appoint a man or men in consultation with the director of elementary education to edit school books and prepare them for printing. All manuscripts must be sent to the chairman of the school board for revision.

6. The State Publishers see to the printing and forwarding of the school books. The number and sizes of the books to be decided in consultation with the director of elementary education.

7. The Minister of Education has the final word in all discussions.

In 1941 a law was passed amending the law of 1930 establishing Secondary Schools in rural areas. This law provided for four additional towns to have such Secondary Schools:

Siglufjordur.   Seydisfjordur.
Nordfjordur.   Akranes.

CHAIN OF ADMINISTRATION
IN THE ICELANDIC SCHOOL SYSTEM

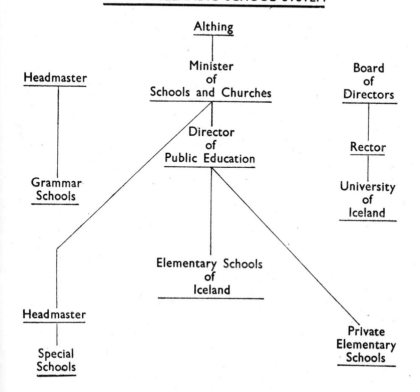

CHAPTER V

GRAMMAR SCHOOLS

There are only two Grammar Schools in Iceland; one in
Reykjavik and one in Akureyri. The Grammar School in
Reykjavik is the oldest school in the country. It was originally
founded at the Bishopric of Holar in the year 1107 by Bishop
Jon Ogmundsson who also built the Catholic Cathedral Church
in Reykjavik. In this early school was taught Latin, poetry
and music in preparation for the priesthood. A year later
another school was founded at Skalholt by Isleif Gissursson,
son of Gizur the White, who built the first church at Skalholt.
These schools were called Latin Schools, evidently because the
chief subject was Latin. Only educated men attended these

schools, since they were the only ones who were capable of speaking and writing that language. The Latin School at Holar was discontinued from 1203 to 1237, at which time it was re-opened and continued up to 1341, when it was again discontinued. The school at Skalholt had closed down about 1246. These schools were re-opened in 1557 by royal decree as previously stated.

In 1783 steps were taken to remove the bishop's seat and the Latin School at Skalholt to Reykjavik, and this measure was carried out in 1785. In 1841 the schools at Holar and Skalholt were united into one Latin School located at Reykjavik. The headmaster at this time was Jon Jonsson. A certificate from this school gave the right of ordination.

During the 1804–05 period this school was not in operation, due to the Napoleonic Wars. This school, for a few years, was at Holavellir in Reykjavik and then at Bessastadir, the residence of the present Regent of Iceland.

The subjects taught in the early Latin Schools were Icelandic, religion, catechism and arithmetic. The Grammar School did not become divided into the present-day divisions until 1909, at which time the name of the school became Mentaskolinn. The school was divided into two divisions; higher and lower. The reasons for the two divisions are apparent.

The lower division of the Icelandic Grammar School is two years in length and is a general course. The higher division is divided into two branches; the language branch and the mathematics branch. The student selects the branch coinciding with his choice of life work. The student with moderate funds may take the lower division of two years and leave the school with a general education, while the student in better circumstances and the student intending to enter a profession continues into the higher division.

The Grammar School in Reykjavik has nineteen teachers. The one in Akureyri has fifteen teachers. Most of the textbooks used in these schools are Danish and Icelandic. Many progressive steps have been made since the early date, and many of the outstanding men of the country have graduated from them.

In 1937 the rules governing the Grammar Schools were revised, modified and modernized by the Parliament. The entrance requirements were specifically set forth in this new law and were as follows:

1. The student must be able to read prose and poetry and know Icelandic grammar.

2. He must be able to write a short essay on any selected subject and express himself well.

3. He must be able to write a legible hand.

4. He must have a knowledge of arithmetic.

5. He must have read at least 150 pages of Danish and be able to translate any given page that has been read.

6. He must know Icelandic history and the main points of world history.

7. He must know Icelandic geography and European geography.

8. He should know and identify birds and plants of Iceland, as well as having a knowledge of birds and plants of other countries.

After passing the above entrance requirements the student enters the lower division of the Grammar School, which consists of two years. The courses and hours in each as prescribed by Parliament are as follows:

		Hours per week 1st year	Hours per week 2nd year
1.	Icelandic	5	4
2.	Danish	0	4
3.	English	5	5
4.	Arithmetic	5	5
5.	History	3	3
6.	Natural History	4	4
7.	Geography	5	2
8.	Physics	0	3
9.	Drawing	2	2
10.	Gymnastics	3	3

A total of 35 hours per week each year. The students spend, therefore, thirty-five hours per week in classroom.

Each grammar school class has a teacher-advisor appointed by the headmaster of the school for the term. This advisor must know each student and keep abreast of his conduct and progress and make reports to the headmaster, who in turn advises the parents or guardians on matters of school progress and health of the individual. Each class also has a student inspector whose job it is to supervise conduct and scholastic matter of the class, and to act in behalf of the class with school authorities.

After graduation from the lower or two-year division the student may enter the higher division of four years. The first year of the higher division of the school all students take the same courses and same number of hours in each course. At the beginning of the second year of the higher division the student must select his major; either languages or mathematics. After this selection is made all students continue to take the same subjects, but the hours spent on each subject will vary.

At the end of each year a final examination is given, and if more students pass than can be accommodated in the next class only the ones with the highest marks are accepted. Within the class, examinations, which count in the final average, are given in December and March. Marks in religion, bookkeeping and drawing do not count in this average. A student may come up for any of the examinations, without having attended the classes, with the proper testimonials from his teachers. All final examinations are given by the teachers of the school and outside censors especially selected by the Board of Education. These teachers and censors select the examination questions.

If the student does not receive satisfactory marks in the examinations held in December and March he is not allowed to take the final examination for the year. The final mark in a subject is the average of the teachers' marks on the bi-yearly examinations plus the average received in the final examination. A passing mark is fifty per cent., but a zero in any one subject fails the student for the year.

In 1940 there was a total of two hundred and fifty-eight students in the Grammar School at Reykjavik. Fifty-five of them were in the lower division and two hundred and three in the higher. Forty-eight students graduated from the school in 1940.

For comparison, the Icelandic Grammar Schools would be equal to the American College. Graduates of the Reykjavik and Akureyri Grammar Schools (colleges) are eligible to enter the University of Iceland and universities in North, Middle and Western Europe for scientific education.

Before the war approximately 200 Icelandic graduates each year who had all studied at these colleges were studying in various universities in Europe; most of them in universities in the Scandinavian countries—Denmark, Sweden and Norway; some in Germany, France and Britain.

This standing (graduate of these colleges) has for a long time been recognized by most European universities as equal to that of their own preparatory schools (Gymnasias, Lycées and Grammar Schools), and Icelandic graduates can enter these universities to study whatever scientific course they wish without taking any special college courses.

For quite some time the Icelandic government has yearly aided, with parliamentary grants, a number of promising scholars to continue their studies at universities in other countries.

The University of Iceland in Reykjavik

HOURS PER WEEK IN EACH SUBJECT IN THE HIGHER DIVISION OF
GRAMMAR SCHOOL

	1st year	2nd year		3rd year		4th year	
		Lang.	Math.	Lang.	Math.	Lang.	Math.
Icelandic ..	4	3	3	3	3	3	3
Danish ..	3	3	3	0	0	0	0
English ..	4	4	4	4	0	5	0
German ..	4	3	3	3	3	4	3
French ..	0	0	0	6	5	6	5
Latin ..	0	6	4	6	0	7	0
History ..	3	3	3	3	4	3	0
Religion ..	1	0	0	0	0	0	0
Natural History ..	0	3	3	3	4	3	4
Physics and Chemistry	4	3	4	0	6	0	7
Mathematics..	4	3	4	3	6	0	7
Astronomy ..	0	0	0	0	0	0	2
Book-keeping	2	0	0	0	0	0	0
Drawing ..	2	0	0	0	0	0	0
Gymnastics ..	3	3	3	3	3	3	3
Music ..	1	1	1	1	1	1	1
Total ..	35	35	35	35	35	35	35

CHAPTER VI

UNIVERSITY OF ICELAND

The first step of what eventually resulted in a University of Iceland began with the establishment of a Theological Seminary (Prestaskoli Islands) in 1847, with two years' curriculum. This Divinity School became the present theological faculty of the University. The origin of this seminary can be traced to the schools started by a vote of the Althing in the year 1000 and headed by different learned men and priests. This was soon after Christianity was accepted as the official faith. The first headmaster of the Theological Seminary was Peter Petersson, later a bishop. The subjects taught were: Church History, Ethics, Doctrinal Theology, Sermon Writing and Pastoral Theology.

The second step toward a University was made in 1876 when a Medical Faculty (Laeknaskoli Islands) was established by an act of the Althing. This faculty was established because of the great need for doctors, few in number at the time.   Before this medical faculty was established medical students had to go to the University of Copenhagen to complete their studies.   In fact, they had to continue to go to the University of Copenhagen for obstetrics until 1930, when the State Hospital (Landsspitals) opened.

Gudmundur Magnusson was one of the first teachers of the Medical School and was later Dean.   He was one of Iceland's most successful surgeons.   It was also due to his efforts and leadership that ethical standards of the medical profession were set up.

The third step toward the University was made in 1908 when the Law School of Iceland (Lagaskoli Islands) was founded by an act of the Althing.   This school was inaugurated October 1, 1908.   The first dean (forstodumadur) was the late Larus H. Bjarnason, later Professor Juris of the University of Iceland and thereafter Judge of the Supreme Court of Iceland.   The first, and at that time only, instructor (kennari) was Einar Arnorsson, later Professor Juris and now Judge of the Supreme Court. Eight students were admitted to the law school during the first term.   It was housed at Thingholtsstraeti 26, Reykjavik during its short life of three years.   There are no graduates of this law school because it was merged with the University when that was founded by an act of the Parliament on June 17, 1911.   This law school faculty became the Law Faculty of the University with three professors.   Larus H. Bjarnason was the first chairman of the law faculty.   The faculty held its meetings at the Althingishus (House of Parliament) until the University moved to its new building.   The subjects taught at the law school were:

1. Civil Law I (Family Law, Personal Rights, Wills, etc.).
2. Civil Law II (Commercial Law, Real Property, Mortgages, etc.).
3. Criminal Law (Slander).
4. Civil and Criminal Procedure (Law of Evidences, Law Courts, etc.).
5. Constitutional and International Law.
6. History of the law, particularly the ancient laws of Iceland.

These three schools were brought together and the University of Iceland was founded on the birthday of Jon Sigurdsson, the liberator of Iceland.   The first session of the University was held in the parliament building, and it continued there until 1940, when a new, modernistic building was erected from funds derived from a National Lottery.   This new building containing the

University is a nucleus for a larger University, as a large expansion and building programme is under way. In order to enter the University one must be a graduate of the grammar schools.

The University at the present time has four faculties: Theology, with six instructors; Medicine, with thirteen instructors; Philosophy, representing Icelandic Philology and History, Psychology, Logic, Pedagogy, English, German, French, Swedish, Italian, Spanish and the corresponding literatures, with ten instructors; Law, with six instructors; and Economics, with nine instructors. The Law and Economics courses are contained in one faculty. For those students going abroad for further study Mathematics, Physics, Chemistry, Statics and Technical Drawing are given as a basis for advanced study.

Some of the instructors in the Medical Department are practising physicians in Reykjavik and some law instructors are also lawyers in Reykjavik. Icelandic literature is stressed very much at the University. The Eddas and Sagas hold equally important places in the literature course and receive the major part of the instruction time. The predominant thought of the University is to train its students along conservative lines. Political thought among the students is encouraged and stimulated by means of student organizations. All students are required to take eighty lessons of gymnastics and forty lessons of swimming each year. The only exceptions to this requirement are those physically incapacitated. In the 1941-42 school year two hundred and sixty-two men and forty-two women attended the University, of which twenty-two were graduated. The average graduation age is twenty-seven.

The University of Iceland is administered by a Board of Directors. This board is composed of the Dean from each faculty and the Rector of the University. It passes on new instructors and other administrative problems. In hiring new instructors the Board of Directors is most interested in the prospective faculty member's research, technical studies and written theses, either published or to be published. All degrees and higher study are taken into consideration by a committee, of three to five members, taken from the Board of Directors. The confirmation is by the State Minister of Education.

In 1941 an act of the Althing created a department of Dentistry within the Medical Faculty in the University. This law stated that a student to be qualified to pursue Dentistry must have completed the pre-medical course in the Medical Faculty. The law provided for a regular instructor and a dental technician, the latter to also act as instructor.

PART III

General Education

THE TEACHERS' TRAINING SCHOOL

"KENNARASKOLINN"

Iceland has had an institution for training teachers since 1892. At its founding, by a clergyman, it was part of a grammar school. In 1908 it was made a separate school maintained by the State. To-day approximately ninety students attend the school each year.

The purpose of the Teachers' Training School has always been only to train teachers for the elementary schools of Iceland. As is the case with all schools of the country, and many other countries, it has developed gradually and along conservative lines. Let us see the curriculum as it was in 1908 and compare it with the curriculum of the 1942–43 school year.

1908	1942–43
Icelandic	Icelandic
Danish	Danish
Icelandic and World History	Icelandic and World History
Geography	Geography
Arithmetic	Mathematics (this included arithmetic and geometry)
Writing	Writing
Drawing	Drawing
Handicraft	Handicraft
Religion	Religion
Singing	Singing
Gymnastics (in the early days this included Health)	Gymnastics
Natural History	Natural History
Psychology of Education[1] (this included the Science of Teaching)	

[1] This has always been a course in child development from infancy to adolescence.

46

Teachers' Training School in Reykjavik

1908	1942-43
Practice Teaching	Practice Teaching
	English
	Biology
	Bible History
	Physics and Chemistry (combined)
	Health
	Swimming

From examination of the curriculum of the school one may see that it is not overloaded with non-essentials. Emphasis has been, and is, placed on the study of Icelandic. Algebra was offered at one time some years ago but was discontinued. Other courses have come and gone after a short time in the same manner. For example: Geology was offered at one time but was soon dropped. The reason for this was that some teacher at the school was interested and qualified to teach this particular subject and obtained permission from the headmaster of the school to offer the course for one period each week, for a short time, during the term. If the teacher left the school, or time did not permit, the course was dropped.

The first new course to be offered was Biology in 1912. The text was Danish, but was later translated into Icelandic. To-day the course in Biology is a part of Natural History but has a separate text. The next course to be added was Bible History in 1920. In 1924 English was added. One of the teachers at the Teachers' Training School, who was also a member of Parliament, presented and debated the proposition of adding English, giving as his reason for this addition the expansion of trade with England and the consequent need for the language. He foresaw the power of the English-speaking nations. Another reason was to keep abreast of the grammar school, which had offered English for some years.

In 1925 Physics and Chemistry were added and, in the same year, Health was made a separate subject. The last addition to the curriculum was Swimming, which was added in 1942. Swimming is now taught as a required subject in elementary schools where a swimming pool is available.[1] The amount of Practice Teaching has been increased by one-half since the beginning of the school.

The regulations governing the Teachers' Training School have been changed only three times during the school's existence.

[1] Most elementary schools in larger towns and villages have indoor pools, or have outdoor pools which are used the entire year, due to the fact that Iceland has many hot springs which are used to feed these pools.

In 1908, when the school was set up as a separate institution; again in 1924; and in 1934. At the present time it is planned to add an additional year to the school, making it a four-year course to receive a certificate to teach. This change will require another revision of the regulations.

One reason for such a conservative programme is the reluctance on the part of school boards to urge or sanction new teaching methods, or to add new subjects to the school's curriculum in order to keep pace with the progress of the country. Another reason may be the spirit of complacency due to the fact that the people as a whole have been able to read and write since early times, as the Sagas òf the country bear witness. Since this was gained in the homes why should the schools be developed much more than at their beginning?

The Icelandic Teachers' Training School has among its formal courses "Uppeldisfraedi," or literally translated "Psychology of Learning." The text used deals wholly with the mental development of the child from infancy to adolescence. No books on Educational Psychology have been written by Icelandic writers, so a book by an Austrian writer has been translated and is used. More stress is put on child development than on the learning processes.

Aside from the course in Psychology, the Teachers' Training School has one other course which deals with teaching as a profession. This course is "Kennslufraedi," which translated means "Methods of Teaching." This course has developed gradually and up until 1931 was taught in connection with Psychology of Education.

The training school has three instructors who act as teacher trainers in the elementary school, which is run in connection with the Teachers' Training School. The Methods of Teaching course is both lecture and practical work. One of the student-teacher supervisors may take arithmetic, geography and religion as courses in which he gives lectures. During the last year of the student's training he is supervised in regular classroom work in the elementary training school. Here the student has the class and conducts the work under the supervision of the instructor.

The lectures in the Methods of Teaching course deal mostly with classroom poise and other classroom techniques that an experienced teacher has gained by teaching. These techniques are then put into practice. The student or apprentice teacher gets twenty-five hours of actual practice teaching before graduation from the Teachers' Training School. No textbook is used in this course. All teaching is based on actual experience of the instructors.

A small amount of psychological research in the schools has been done during the past ten years and a few results of such research have been published. However, no changes have taken place in the method of instruction nor any specific conclusions drawn from the research. At this time no psychologists are employed in the schools of Iceland, due to the lack of trained personnel for such work.

In 1933 an examination for all elementary school pupils in the entire country was started.[1] This examination is given annually in the spring and is for the purpose of making comparisons, between schools, as to progress. It, or rather the studied results, have to some extent been used to determine the efficiency of teachers throughout the country. As for more detailed study of methods of teaching and classroom results in various subjects these examinations have not been used. However, they are filed from year to year.

The elementary school pupils are examined in arithmetic, reading, geography, natural science and history. Each subject has about fifty questions, which range from simple questions to more difficult ones, thus embracing a wide range of knowledge. These examinations are marked in the school by specially appointed censors and forwarded to the office of the Director of Public Elementary Education, where they are examined for error and filed.

It has been found, from studies of these examinations, that pupils in general have a very thorough background of the essential subjects needed for a general education. It was concluded, however, that arithmetic should be given more attention and more thorough methods used in the future.

On the whole the teachers in the Icelandic Elementary Schools are close to middle age; the average age for the four hundred and sixty teachers in the country being approximately forty years. The reason for this advanced age is the fact that the Teachers' Training School trains only for the elementary school. Thus, once embarked on a teaching career in the elementary school, it is the exception when the teacher leaves the elementary field. The graduate from the Teachers' Training School is not eligible to become a teacher in the grammar schools. This can only be done by graduation from a grammar school and by taking additional courses at the University of Iceland.

Out of the eighteen teachers at the Teachers' Training School all have at some time studied at higher institutions abroad. Twelve of these teachers have taken full formal courses. Eight

[1] Suspended for the duration in 1942 due to high cost of paper and shortage of labour.

E

of them have studied in Denmark, three in Germany and one in Scotland. The rest have taken their formal courses in Iceland with shorter courses in foreign universities.

Little counsel is given the student upon entrance to the Training School. Some may be turned away, after a conference with the headmaster and some of the teaching staff, as being unsuitable for future teachers. However, no measuring tests or vocational interest tests are used. The majority of students that fail to enter the school are those failing the entrance examinations which are required of all students.

The students of the school have a Speech Club, which students interested in speech, oratory and dramatics join. This group meets twice monthly, giving speeches which are criticized by members of the club. Part of the evening is devoted to dancing. The membership dues are used by the members at the end of the school year to take a trip about the country. The only other organization in the student body is a choir. Members of this group meet and sing national songs for their recreation. Many of the members sing in local church choirs. The church choirs in Iceland are greatly stressed and are a thing of pride, and much of the outstanding music of the country is choir music. The student body of the Teachers' Training School present one dramatic play each year, late in the winter. This play is in a light vein and attended by the student body, members of the faculty and guests of the actors. It is usually coached by a member of the Reykjavik Theatre Guild.

The teacher of the Icelandic Elementary Schools will, in the near future, bring about many changes. Fortunately the daily schedule of the elementary school is very elastic, thus allowing the teacher to follow lines of good instruction rather than the older, time-bound traditional methods. Present day teachers criticize the teaching of foreign languages[1] in the elementary school, feeling that the average elementary pupil is unable to make proper progress, and that the mother tongue[2] should be known thoroughly first before learning any other language. Another point that is to be settled soon is the use of written examinations more than the traditional European oral examinations. The teachers voice the opinion that the written examination is more fair to the student and that it gives the teacher a better knowledge of the student over a wider range of subject matter.

[1] Danish is taught to twelve-year-old elementary pupils; English to the more diligent pupils of the same age.

[2] Since the occupation of Iceland by American and British forces it is felt that the slang expressions peculiar to both countries might impregnate the pure Icelandic tongue through its youth. Therefore, teachers stress the learning of the mother tongue.

SCHOOLS SET-UP

University of Iceland
Theology
Medicine
Philosophy
Law

Exam.

Grammar School
(Latin School)
4-yrs. 2-div.
Math. and Lang.

Exam.

Grammar School
(Latin School)
2-yrs.
Alg., Geo., Geog.,
Bio., Physics,
Hist. of Iceland
and the World

Exam.

Children's School
Compulsory for all
between 7 and 14
Arith., Reading,
Writing, Danish,
Eng., Geog., Bio. of
Animals, Hist. of
Iceland

Commercial School
Language
Bookkeeping
Econ. Ice. Cor.
Commercial Cal.

Technical School
Icelandic
Mathematics
Gen. Science

Agricultural School
Crops
Livestock

Nautical School
Navigation

Marine Eng. School
Marine Engines

Secondary School
General Educ.
Graduation does not
permit entry to
Latin School or
University

Household School
Trains girls for
homemakers

Training College for
Teachers in Ele-
mentary Schools
Practice and Train.

State Horticulture
School
Greenhouses
Garden Crops

School of Music

School for the Blind

School for Deaf-mute
Children

One must compliment the Icelandic Elementary School teachers on the enthusiasm they have for their work. They are well aware of their responsibility. They know that the direction of the learning in the new generation determines the future of their country. For Iceland, the oldest Republic in the world, this means the continuation of freedom and justice and a country that will be a good neighbour in the brotherhood of nations after the war.

TEACHERS' TRAINING SCHOOL FOR TEACHERS OF SPORTS AND GYMNASTICS

A Teachers' Training School for teachers of sports and gym nastics in the schools of Iceland was established in 1942 by an act of Althing. This school is located inland near a lake and hot springs. The purpose of such a school is to instruct men and women in the teaching of gymnastics and sports in the schools and in Health Societies.

The subjects taught are: Gymnastics (exercises), swimming, free sports, ball playing (this included football), popular sports of Iceland, skiing, skating, rowing and sailing.

The theoretical courses are: Icelandic language and literature, physiology, the science of teaching and chemistry.

First aid includes the study of sports in relation to the human body, psychology and the science of education.

Sportsmanship, good conduct, abstinence, rules of different games and the construction of playing fields, swimming pools and stadiums are also among the subjects.

The school term is nine months, beginning in October and ending in June. The school is divided into two departments. One for the training of teachers in the schools and the other to train amateur athletes and leaders for Health Societies of the country.

A board of three is set up for the school. One member will be the State Supervisor of Sport for Iceland, who will act as Chairman, one member is appointed by the Ministry of Education, and the third member will be the headmaster of the district school of Laugarvatn, in which district and building this new school is located.

The school has a headmaster and two teachers. The salaries are the same as for the teachers in the regular Teachers' Training School in Reykjavik. Other rules as to appointment and dismissal of teachers will be the same as in other district schools of the country.

As this school is new the Ministry of Education has not yet issued any regulations.

Merchants' Commercial School

MERCHANTS' COMMERCIAL SCHOOL
"Verslunarskolinn"

In 1905 the leading merchants of Reykjavik started a Commercial School. The reason for this school was that formerly any business training the Icelandic people had was obtained abroad. The men most responsible for this school were: Olafur C. Eyjolfsson, the first headmaster of the school; Dithlef Thomsen, Danish Consul and merchant of Reykjavik at this time; and B. H. Bjarnason, merchant of Reykjavik.

During the first year of the school's existence 54 students attended, the second year 66 attended and during 1940 a total of 85 students attended.

The school is supported, in part, by funds from the Merchants' Society. Each merchant pays annual dues to this society. The balance of the maintenance of the school is paid by the State and by fees paid by the students. This school is a private, co-educational institution. The fees to attend are 250 kronur ($37.50) per year exclusive of room and board. The staff consists of one headmaster, fifteen teachers and five school board members. The subjects taught are Icelandic, English, German, Spanish, Danish, Commercial Law, Economics, Commercial History, Commercial Geography, Political Science, Mathematics, History of Iceland, Bookkeeping, Vorufraedi (A Science of Industrial Things), Typewriting, Shorthand (Danish). In teaching languages foreign periodicals and magazines are used. For the English class the *English Observer*, the *Manchester Guardian*, the *Reader's Digest, Strand Magaziue*, and *Britannia and Eve* are used.

The Commercial School has, in all, six years. This is broken down as follows: one year is a preliminary class which usually accepts fifty students per year; the course proper which is four years in length; the student can go further with his studies and take an additional post-graduate course of one year. Entrance is from fourteen to sixteen years of age. Each student must take an entrance examination which is as follows: Icelandic, reading, writing and grammar; English; Danish; Arithmetic and Penmanship.

The purpose of the preliminary class of one year is to prepare students to take the regular four-year course, especially those students coming directly from the elementary school. There is no entrance examination for the preliminary class. The fifth year or the post-graduate course is mostly Economics. The teachers are both part-time and regular teachers. The regular teachers are those who have studied abroad and graduated from foreign universities. The part-time teachers are outstanding business men of Reykjavik.

Here are the contents, in brief, of some of the courses a student pursues in the Commercial School. In commercial geography "The Northern Countries in World Economy" is studied. In political science, a study is made of the different forms of government throughout the world. A study is made of the Icelandic government. A thorough study of the Althing, the voting powers and the right to vote in Iceland, is made.

Upon leaving the Commercial School a rather difficult final examination is taken. This covers Icelandic grammar and literature and writing an essay on one of three subjects offered. The commercial history, commercial geography and political science courses are given in one examination and examples of questions are:

What are the teachings of Karl Marx and Adam Smith?

Write a short essay on slaves all over the world and how slavery was abolished.

What are the most important colonies of France, Great Britain and Italy in Africa?

How were these colonies acquired?

How is Austria connected with Germany?

Write the political history of Germany from Bismarck to Hitler.

When was independence declared in the United States of America?

What are the main raw materials and industries of Europe?

The examination in bookkeeping covers many questions concerning all phases of the subject. This examination is the most difficult. The final examination taken in English comes from books the students have not studied in the regular course. One particular book the English examination sometimes is taken from is *Across Iceland* by Olive Murray Chapman, also the *Hundred Per Cent Office* by Casson.

The majority of the students who attend the Commercial School come from Reykjavik. However, students from other parts of Iceland do attend.

The fees to attend the school are approximately 250 kronur ($38.00) per year, exclusive of board and room. The school year lasts from September to June.

In 1942 the Ministry of Education issued a regulation extending the scope of the Merchants' Commercial School.

1. A department is to be established, the graduates of which may receive a diploma enabling them to attend the University

of Iceland. The diploma will carry the same privileges as a diploma from the grammar schools.

2. The subjects offered in this new department will be:

Icelandic	Latin
German	Danish
English	History
French	Statistics
Mathematics	Natural Science
Science of Government	Bookkeeping and Accounting

Production and Goods of Trade (including Chemistry and Physics).

3. This addition will be a two-year course over the regular school course.

	Hours per week each year	
	1st year	2nd year
Icelandic	2	2
English	5	4
German	2	2
French	5	5
Latin	4	0
Danish	1	0
History	2	2
Production of Goods, etc.	4	4
Mathematics	5	5
Bookkeeping and Accounting	2	2
Statistics and Science of Government	2	2
Total hours	34	28

The student must further fill the demands of the school in music and gymnastics.

In order to qualify for entrance into this higher department the student must graduate from the Commercial School and must have taken the following subjects:

Icelandic	16 hrs.	Geography	6 hrs.
English	19 ,,	Statistics	4 ,,
German	14 ,,	Commercial Law	4 ,,
Danish	14 ,,	History	8 ,,
Bookkeeping	15 ,,	Science of Government	1 ,,
Arithmetic and Mathematics	15 ,,	Production of Goods of Trade	2 ,,

The student must further have satisfied the school demands in typewriting, shorthand, penmanship and gymnastics.

The course in Production and Goods of Trade embodies chemistry, physics, zoology, botany (elementary), and geology with emphasis on Icelandic natural resources and manufactured goods.

The course in history will embody a general world history of main events and men and the parts played by each, the sources of history, the interpretation of historical events, with emphasis on political and economical events of recent times.

In order for the student to enter the upper department of the Commercial School he must have made marks in the regular course better than passing or 5·67.

This school is lenient in its attendance as are all other schools of the country. The student is not required to attend classes in order to take the final examination. If he shows evidence that he has read extensively and studied at home, or that he has been tutored privately, he presents a letter to this effect to the examining board and head master of the school.

Yearly examinations are held usually at the close of the term. The student may take both years of the school in one year if he is capable, however, he must wait for two years to appear for the final examination. If more than five years have elapsed since graduation from the Commercial School he may be required to take the final examinations over again, either all subjects or part. In advancing from the first year to the second year the marks are not required to be as high, 4·25, as for the final examination at the end of the course.

The marks are awarded according to the Orsted system.[1] The final examination is to show if the pupil has acquired information the faculty deems necessary for the student to study at higher schools.

Both written and oral examinations are required in English, Icelandic, Danish and German. · The student is required to write a short composition in all languages taken in the school on two or three selected topics.

All other subjects carry an oral examination only: however, the headmaster may substitute a written examination if he chooses. The oral examination in each subject may be one or two questions.

Two censors are to be present at all examinations.

[1] The Orsted system of marking is a Danish system used in early Icelandic schools. It emphasized wide knowledge and penalized limited knowledge. This system of marking is not used in the Icelandic schools any longer; the decimal system is now used.

Commercial School of the Co-operative Society

CO-OPERATIVE SOCIETY COMMERCIAL SCHOOL

"SAMVINNISKOLINN"

This Commercial School had its beginning in Akureyri in 1916, when a short course was conducted offering bookkeeping and lectures on the co-operative movement. The school was moved to Reykjavik in 1918. The chief promoter of the school was Jonas Jonsson, member of the Althing, who also was the school's first headmaster and is the leader of the Progressive Party.

The purpose of this school is to train young people to operate the co-operative units throughout the country. In fact, the co-operative units engage in practically all managerial and buying pursuits. The first co-operative society started in 1882 on the north-east coast. To-day these stores are found in all parts of the country.

Courses offered at this school are: bookkeeping, arithmetic, English, Icelandic, commercial geography, history of co-operatives, economics, typing, and various lectures and discussions; offered in 1918 as compared with commercial law, German, arithmetic, bookkeeping, English, Swedish or Danish (only Danish now), Icelandic, economics, sociology, history of co-operatives, writing, typing, commercial geography and gymnastics; offered now.

The school has thirty hours' instruction per week and is two years in length.

In the last class there were 50 students, 20 were in the graduating class. The entrance requirements are only to be a graduate of a secondary school.

Social life consists of dances, ball games, swimming and skiing parties.

The students are those who will enter the co-operative movement, and the majority come from rural areas. They come to the school as adults, which helps the social well-being of the school and the co-operative movement.

HOUSEHOLD SCHOOL FOR GIRLS

"KVENNESKOLINN"

The first attempt to found a Secondary, or commonly called Household School, for girls was made at Blondas in 1828 by Bjorn Sigfusson of Kornea. The school was first held at Undirfell Farm, then at Laekjamot Farm, and later at Hof Farm. In 1883 the two counties Skagafjardarsysla and Hunavatnssysla merged their girls' schools and bought the farm of Ytriey as a seat for the combined schools. At this time Elin Briem, an untiring worker for better education for women, became headmistress.

At the beginning of the century a new school house was built at Blondas; at which place the school has remained to the present time.

This school is financed by the State and district besides having a small fee of 100 kronur ($15.00) per student for the term.

During the early years this school was a combined general-education and domestic-science school. In 1928 the school was converted to all domestic science. Practical work is stressed and the school has a model home and garden where the girls receive training. In addition to domestic training—Icelandic, Danish, arithmetic and music is included in the course of study. The term is from September 15th to June 25th.

In 1897 the first Household School was founded in Reykjavik, called Husstjornarskolinn i Reykjavik. Here again we find the work of Elin Briem, now Elin Briem Jonsson. She collected money to found this school. The first teacher and headmistress was Holmfrithur Gisladottir. In 1901, due to financial difficulties, Elin Jonsson gave the school to an Icelandic Agricultural Society which ran it until 1907, at which time Holmfrithur Gisladottir again took the school. This school is still in existence to-day, and is both a boarding- and day-school for girls. It specializes in home-making and needlecraft. It is now financed by the State.

On October 1, 1874, a secondary school or Household School for girls, Kvenneskolinn, was founded in Reykjavik by Thora Melsted, wife of Paul Melsted, well-known teacher in the Latin School. She had already, in 1851, made an attempt to establish such a school with the aid of her sister, Augusta, but it was not until 1871 that her attempt was recognized by prominent citizens in Reykjavik, with the result that it was officially founded at the above-mentioned date.

Thora Melsted, while visiting in Norway, conceived the idea of improving the status of girls who would eventually become housekeepers. From this start the Household Schools of Iceland have become important institutions and serve well a very important need.

To gain a financial start she wove a multi-coloured rug which sold for 200 kronur ($30.00).

In 1875 the school received financial aid of 200 kronur ($30.00) from the State, and it has received 1,500 kronur ($225.00) per year since.

Only 34 girls attended the first year. At the present time approximately 130 girls attend each year.

Thora Melsted conducted the school for 32 years. When she resigned Ingibjorg H. Bjarnason took her place and conducted the school until her death in 1941, a total of 35 years. Up to the present time about three thousand girls have graduated from this school.

Girls may enter this school as young as 13 years of age. After taking the regular course the student, to get training in cooking, must spend an additional four to six months. The regular course included the following subjects:

Icelandic	Geology
Danish	Sociology
Swedish	Bookkeeping and Typing
English	Drawing
German	Writing
Icelandic History	Sewing and Dressmaking
Geography	Embroidery Work
Mathematics	Knitting
Natural History	Nursing
Hygiene	Gymnastics
Physics	Swimming
Chemistry	

Headmistresses of the school were:
Thora Melsted, from 1874 until 1906.
Ingibjorg H. Bjarnason, from 1906 until 1942.
Ragnherdur Jonsdottir, from 1942 until —.

In 1941 the law which established the Household Schools in rural areas was changed, making it possible for the State to pay three-fourths of the establishing cost of these schools in country districts, or to take over three-fourths of the establishing debts of previously established schools.

In 1941 the Althing passed a law broadening the powers of establishing Household Schools. The provisions of the law were:

1.   Household Schools to be established in towns whenever money was made available by city and state.

2.   The purpose of such schools will be to teach girls, in theory and practice, to do all the usual household duties and to manage a home.

3.   The entrance age to be not less than 16 years of age. The term to be seven months for one or two years.

4.   Subjects: Icelandic, Cooking, Child Care, Household Account Keeping, Handicraft and Home Work, Hygiene, Nursing, Gardening and Child Development.

5.   Each school will have a board of five members. The Minister of Education will act as chairman and the other members

will be appointed by the local town council. They will serve for four years.

6. The headmistresses and teachers will be appointed by the Ministry of Education in consultation with the board of education of the school.

7. The State will pay three-fourths of the cost of establishing the school and so much for each student according to the number of students.

8. No fees are to be charged the students.

9. Each school will have space for a garden. If the school is to be a boarding school the cost must not exceed 40 kronur ($6.00) per year.

10. A Household Teachers' Training School may be established in connection with the Household School in Reykjavik.

11. The provisions of this law are to coincide with the laws of 1938 establishing such Household Schools in the rural areas of the country.

CHAPTER II

Special Education

NAVIGATION SCHOOL

In 1869 a committee of three men, Erikur Briem, Sigurdur Stefansson and Thorsteinn Jonsson, was appointed by the Althing to draft provisions for the founding of a school for seamen. In 1890 a Nautical School was established by an act of the Althing.

This school, however, was not the first such training school for seamen. The very first nautical school was carried on by an old fisherman, Torfi Halldorsson, at Isyerfjordur in 1852. This school gave seamen and fishermen training in navigation only. Besides this first nautical school there were others up until the one established by the Althing in Reykjavik.

The present one has had three headmasters. All have been seamen of wide experience. The first headmaster was Markus Bjarnason, the second Pall Halldarsson and the present one Fridereik Olafsson.

This school is fully financed by the State, the only cost to the student is for books and living expenses. The school has fifteen instructors and an average attendance of from 70 to 80 students each year. The Icelandic fishing fleet, the coastal patrol and the merchant fleet are prohibited by law from signing on any seaman who has not attended this Nautical or the Marine Engineers'

Class in the Household Teachers' Training School

School. The main subjects of all branches of the school are Navigation, Maritime Law and the Icelandic Language.

The Nautical School is divided into the following divisions: the four-month course which gives the student training and the right to operate boats up to 75 tons. The subjects taught in this division are:

1. Mathematics, oral.
   Fundamentals of arithmetic and geometry.

2. Navigation, oral and written.
   Knowledge of the globe, latitude and longitude.
   Knowledge and use of the compass, magnetism and variations of the compass.
   How to use the ship's log.
   Knowledge of sea charts and their uses.
   Principles of making charts.
   How to compute drift and how to set the course of a ship.
   How to locate a ship on the chart.
   Calculation of ebb and tide.
   How to use the sextant to find location on a chart.

3. Seamanship.
   Knowledge of International Navigation Rules.
   Emergency use of signals.
   Use of life-saving devices.
   Knowledge of rigging and tackle of a ship.
   How to use various fishing gear.

4. Icelandic, oral and written.
   The student must have read at least 50 pages of prose and poetry.
   Must be able to explain clearly what was read.
   The subject to be read shall concern nautical terms and knowledge.

5. Maritime Law, Icelandic waters.
   Laws regarding rights and duties of seamen.

6. First Aid.
   The student will be trained to cope with minor accidents and illnesses.
   Must have a knowledge of quarantines.

The above courses are held in the school at Reykjavik. However, in other towns about the country, two-month courses are held yearly entitling those who have attended them to navigate motor boats within 75 tons.

Students desiring to sign on larger ships than 75 tons are required to take a four-month preliminary course, which is separate and apart from the four-month course for those students signing on ships of 75 tons or less.

After completion of the four-month preliminary course the student goes to sea and works for a period of four to six months. He then returns to school for the next higher course which takes six months to complete and gives the right to sign on ships of more than 75 tons as a mate.

This six-month course consists of the following courses:

1. Mathematics.
   Fundamentals of arithmetic and geometry.
   The use of logarithm tables.
   Know how to extract roots.
2. Plane geometry.
3. Trigonometry, sine and cosine.
4. Solid geometry.
5. Navigation.
   Knowledge of the globe, latitude and longitude.
   Knowledge and use of the compass, magnetism and variations of the compass.
   How to use the ship's log.
   Astronomy.
6. Use of radio signals in plotting a ship.
7. Seamanship.
   Knowledge of International Navigation Rules.
   Emergency use of signals.
   Use of life-saving devices.
   Knowledge of rigging and tackle of a ship.
   How to use various fishing tackle and gear.
8. Icelandic.
   Student must have read at least 100 pages of prose and poetry.
   Have a good knowledge of Icelandic grammar.
9. Danish. A speaking knowledge.
10. English. A speaking knowledge.
11. Maritime Law.
    Laws regarding rights and duties of seamen.
12. First Aid.
    Be able to cope with minor accidents and illnesses.
    Knowledge of the rules of quarantines.
13. Bookkeeping. Double entry systems.
14. Knowledge of engines—functions, use and upkeep.

Some of the above subjects are a duplication of the four-month course subjects, but they go into detail more.

After completion of the six-month course the student leaves the school and goes to sea for one to two years to obtain more practical experience. He comes back to school for the final seven-month course which gives him the right to become a captain on merchantmen or trawlers.

This course, seven-month, contains the following:

1. Mathematics.
   A duplication of the six-month course with the addition of algebra.
2. Plane geometry.
3. Solid geometry.
   Navigation.
   Same as the six-month course with the addition of the following:
   > The correction of the compass.
   > How to use sounding devices for depth.
   > Nautical astronomy.
   > Knowledge of the use of the chronometer.
   > The plotting of location of a ship by astronometrical observations.
   > Knowledge of the use of radio in navigation.
5. Knowledge of marine engines.
6. Physics.
7. Seamanship.
   Same as in the six-month course with the addition of:
   > Shipbuilding and construction.
   > Loading and maintenance of ships.
   > Rules and regulations of loading ships.
   > Steering of ships in harbours, channels and the open sea.
   > Use of loading and unloading devices.
   > Safety measures against going aground.
   > Use of lifeboats under all conditions.
   > Use of life-saving devices.
8. Coastal geography of the continental countries and meteorology.
   Knowledge of navigable trade rivers of various countries.
   Know the trade routes of the world.
9. Icelandic. Must be able to read and explain clearly at least 200 pages of prose.
10. Danish. Must be able to read and explain clearly 200 pages.
11. English. Same as for Danish.
12. German. Same as for Danish and English.
13. Maritime Law.

14. First Aid.
15. Bookkeeping.
16. Commercial Economics.

The student in either the six- or the seven-month course does not have to spend all the time required for practical experience at one time. He may spend only a few months at a time at sea and then finish all the schooling required. He may then return to the school and put in the remaining time at sea at a later date to finish out his practical work. After this is done the student may complete the examination for captain. This is the only school in Iceland where practical work and experience are stressed.

Only elementary school education is required for admission to the Nautical School. The prospective student must be able to swim, have good eyesight, have good hearing and have a powerful voice.

Iceland has three coastal patrol boats whose duty is to enforce fishing regulations within Icelandic waters. Students completing the Nautical School may take the examination to become a captain on these ships. However, it is not, as yet, required by law to take this examination as it is for all fishing boats and merchant ships.

The course of instruction for the coastal patrol boats is as follows:

Artillery, operation of range finders and fire control instruments.
Optics, knowledge of prisms and light.
Mathematics and surveying.
International signals.
International maritime law.
English.
Danish.
German.
Icelandic.
Salvage of ships.
Gymnastics.

On the whole the examinations in the Nautical School are very rigid. Each division final examination carries a designated number of points: 104 points in the examination for fishing boats under 75 tons, 168 points for those over 75 tons, 264 points in the examination for Merchant Marine and 96 points for the Coastal Patrol examination. The student must have 50 per cent. of the answers correct to pass any examination.

The Nautical School is expanding rapidly. It will follow the expansion of Iceland's Merchant and Fishing Fleet. Under the able leadership it has enjoyed since its founding its influence will be a leading factor in the efficiency and working conditions of all Icelandic seamen.

The school, at present, has two main objectives, namely a better building with better facilities for instruction and the constant introduction of new methods. It will be the future policy of the school to send each year some of the instructors abroad for new ideas and methods. This year, 1942, the school has one of its instructors attending the University of California.

SUBJECTS AND HOURS IN NAVIGATION SCHOOL

Subjects	For Capt. of boats under 75 tons	For Capt. of boats 75 tons and over and mates of Merchant Marine	2nd year for heavier fishing boats	2nd year for Merchant Marine	3rd year for Merchant Marine	4th year for Coastal Patrol only
Mathematics	5	13	2	3	3	0
Navigation	16	2	10	9	11	0
Icelandic	4	6	4	4	3	0
Danish	0	4	3	2	2	0
English	0	3	3	3	2	3
German	0	0	0	0	0	3
Maritime Law	2	0	2	2	1	0
Hygiene	2	1	1	1	1	0
Bookkeeping	0	0	1	1	1	0
Sc. of Trade	0	0	1	1	1	0
Physics	0	1	1	1	1	0
Engineering	0	0	2	2	2	0
Geography and Meteorology	0	0	1	1	1	0
Seamanship	7	7	7	8	9	0
Gunnery	0	0	0	0	0	5
Sc. of Light	0	0	0	0	0	1
Surveying	0	0	0	0	0	2
International Law	0	0	0	0	0	2
International Signals	0	0	0	0	0	4
Gymnastics	0	1	1	1	1	1
Total	36	38	39	39	39	23

MARINE ENGINEERS' SCHOOL

In 1915, with the expanding use of motor ships, the Althing founded an Engineers' School with special emphasis on marine engines. The first and present headmaster is a Dane, M. E. Jessen, who has had long experience on the sea.

Prior to the founding of this Marine Engineers' School most all engineers on Iceland's boats were Danes. Later many Icelanders went to Denmark to study and returned to the fishing

F

boats; however, it was found most helpful to have a training base in the home country.

For the student to graduate with a certificate from this school he must:

1. Write an easy composition in Icelandic on any subject and have it grammatically correct.

2. Have a knowledge of arithmetic, algebra, proportions, roots, geometry, equations, trigonometry and be able to use surveying instruments.

3. Take a course in physics.

4. Know the principles of all marine engines and their maintenance.
   Know mechanical drawing.

6. Be able to read and translate from a Danish technical book.

7. Be able to read and translate English.

The examinations of this school are both oral and written, Three examiners are appointed by the government; one to be the headmaster of the school, and, of the other two, at least one to have passed an examination in engineering. The government may appoint special examiners in the languages. The oral part of the examination is conducted by the regular teachers.

In order to take the entrance examination to the school the aspirant must have worked three years in a machine shop approved by the government and show a letter from his employer describing his proficiency. Application for entrance to the school must be submitted three months in advance.

Rules and conditions of admittance to this school will be issued and controlled by the government. Those passing the final examination receive a diploma enumerating the subjects taken in the school and the grades received in each. The government appoints a special examination committee to draw up the examination questions.

The school now has the following divisions: the lower engineering division (one-year course), the higher engineering division (two-year course), and the electricity division for engineers and electricians (one-year course for engineers and two-year course for electricians).

The average age at graduation from this school is twenty-four, and all graduates are assured jobs on the fishing trawlers and boats and the Merchant Fleet.

Technical School in Reykjavik

Each year a course in engineering is held by the Fiskifelag Islands at different places in the country where the fishing industry is carried on in a large scale. These courses give the graduate the right to handle motors of 150 horsepower. A higher engineering course is also held by the same society in Reykjavik. Some knowledge in carpentry is necessary to attend this course which gives the graduate the right to handle motors of 400 horsepower. Teachers in these courses are men with long experience in the fishing industry and at sea.

TECHNICAL SCHOOL

In the beginning of the nineteenth century technical progress in Iceland had reached such a stage that it was considered necessary to organize the training of the tradesmen. A technical school was accordingly established in Reykjavik. The chief promoter of this school was Jon Thorlaksson, a civil engineer by profession, who later became Prime Minister of Iceland. The purpose of this school was to give to apprentices theoretical training along with the practical and instil in the young people the pride of being skilled with their hands.

In the beginning this school had few teachers, but these few guided the students into the apprenticeship system of training which is still very strong in Iceland to-day.

The present Technical School has an enrolment of 300 students and 20 teachers. Helgi Eiriksson, an engineer with a degree from Glasgow, has been headmaster since 1932.

The Reykjavik Technical School is maintained as follows: one-fifth State aid, one-third town aid, and the remainder is made up from fees paid by the masters of the trades in which the students are working. It costs 130 kronur ($19.50) a year for a master to have a student attend the Technical School. Before the war, in 1940, the master could send a student to the school for 80 kronur ($12.00). The increase in fees was due to the increase in operating expenses and the increase in teachers' salaries. The school year is seven months long, beginning October 1st and ending the last of April.

At the present time the Technical School does not have any machinery or hand tools. They only have drawing equipment and the rest of the instruction is from textbooks. Plans are drawn and estimates are being taken for a new building. The government has acquired the ground. This new building will be equipped with modern shop machinery and hand tools.

In 1927 the Althing made it compulsory for apprentices to attend the trade school. The trade unions govern the number of apprentices in a trade. The trades are as follows:

Bakers	Milliners
Body Workers (car)	Confectioners
Motor Mechanics	Line Makers
Bookbinders	Painters
Brushmakers	Metal Founders
Gas Fitters	Masons
Goldsmiths	Plumbers
Hair Dressers	Printers
Upholsterers	Telephone Repairers
Cabinet Makers	Electricians
House Builders	Barbers
Blacksmiths	Turners
Kettle Makers	Compositors
Tailors	Shipbuilders
Tinsmiths	Wireless Repairers
Chocolate Makers	Paper Hangers
Watch Makers	Machinists
Shoemakers	

The prospective student for the school must pass an entrance examination. The examination is given on two different days from 7 p.m. to 9 p.m., the usual meeting time of the school.

The entrance examination covers two subjects, Mathematic and Icelandic. The Mathematics examination covers simple additions, subtractions, divisions, fractions and the use of decimals The Icelandic examination consists of a short story read to the student who then writes the story from memory and hands it to the instructor for correction. The story is about 25 printed lines in length, usually about some national event or figure or some well-known folk tale; something similar to the cherry tree incident in the life of Washington or Abe Lincoln's walking five miles to return the change. The purpose of this examination in Icelandic is to test the student's spelling ability and his ability to retain and put into words the thought of the story.

When the master of a trade takes an apprentice each is bound by an agreement. This agreement contains seven sections as follows:

1. The length of the apprenticeship in years.
2. The rate of pay.
3. The master is not allowed to put the apprentice in a hazardous job, or in working conditions injurious to his health.

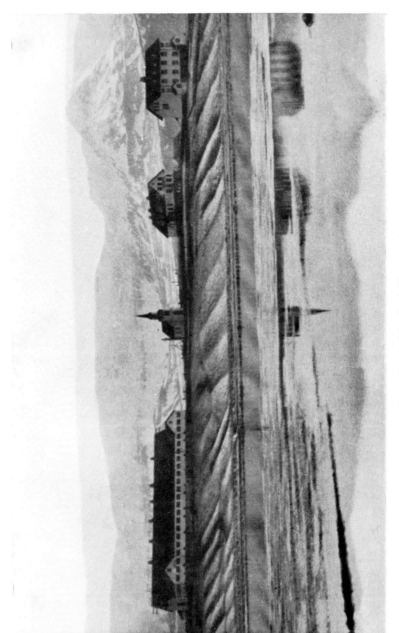

Agricultural School at Hvanneyri

4. The apprentice is to be obedient to the master and take his orders.

4. The master must see that the student attends trade school and gets the necessary education.

6. The master is to teach the apprentice as quickly as possible and see that he makes proper progress in the trade.

7. If, at the end of the apprenticeship period, the student fails the examination, the master must pay the student damages according to a ruling of a board of disinterested persons who investigate the case.

The agreement is signed by the Head of the Police as well as by the representative of the particular trade union to which the agreement pertains. It is also signed by the master and the student-apprentice.

AGRICULTURAL SCHOOLS

In 1880 an Agricultural School was founded by Torfi Bjarnason at Olafsdal. In 1882 another such school was founded in Holar, and another in 1883 at Eidar, and a fourth one in 1903 at Eidum. These schools continued in existence up until 1938, when the number of Agricultural Schools of the country was limited by an act of Althing to two, one on the north coast and one on the south coast.

In 1938 the Althing revised the laws concerning Agricultural Schools and reduced the number to be maintained by the State. The one in the north was to be at Holar and that in the south in Hvanneyri. The purpose was to prepare farmers for their calling. This Act provided:

1. Two schools to be maintained by the State.

2. Farms to be maintained at the seats of the schools at the cost of the State. The headmasters are to manage the farms. Accounts are to be kept. Experiments are to be made in all the branches of farming; cultivation of the soil, horticulture, agriculture (grain-raising), feeding of domestic animals and rotation of crops. The study of the raising of domestic animals is to be as varied as possible in order to find out which kinds are the most profitable.

3. Homesteads may be built in the farmlands by the teachers and workers at the schools at the cost of the State if subsidies are granted in the budget. The Minister of Agriculture to decide the amount of land for the homesteads.

4. One headmaster and two teachers are to be appointed at each school. Salary will be according to the law regulating

the salaries of civil servants. The headmasters are to have
supervision of all things and matters pertaining to the schools
and their buildings. The Minister may grant a sum, equal to the
salaries of two teachers, to each school for theory and practical
teaching. The headmaster appoints two teachers for these
positions with the approval of the Ministry. The regular teachers
may have four months' vacation every six years to study the latest
developments in agriculture. Regular teachers and workers
get one month's vacation each year.

5. The schools to be of three terms, six months each. The
schools to be divided into two departments. Teaching (oral and
from books) to take place chiefly from October 15 to April 15
each year. Instruction in the lower class is to be chiefly from
books; in the upper class, both practical and from books. Pupils
may enter the upper class, if they fulfil all requirements, without
attending the lower class, but such pupils have to stay one year
at the schools.

6. Requirements for entering the schools:
   (a) The pupil is to be 18 years of age. Headmaster may
       grant exceptions.
   (b) Fulfil the requirements, as to knowledge, as stated
       in the regulations.
   (c) Be of good standing (not convicted of any crime) and
       free from contagious diseases.

7. The instruction is to be both from books and practical.
These subjects are to be taught from books:
   (a) Icelandic, arithmetic, geometry, trigonometry, book-
       keeping, sociology, agricultural statistics, history of
       agriculture, Icelandic laws pertaining to agriculture
       as well as such laws of neighbouring countries, com-
       mercial geography, botany, physics, chemistry, geology,
       anatomy and physiology of domestic animals, science
       of domestic animals, science of milk, science of inherit-
       ance, knowledge of tools, science of the cultivation of
       the soil, chief points in house building in rural districts
       and surveying.
   (b) In the upper class a point is to be made of the instruc-
       tion in the science of domestic animals and the culti-
       vation of the soil. Practical knowledge is to be
       imparted at the school farms in the summer between
       the school terms and partly during the last school term.
   (c) Instruction in agricultural occupations to be most
       varied; horticulture, breaking of land, haymaking and
       harvesting, raising of cereals and rotation of crops.

Greenhouses at Hveragerdir Horticultural School

(*d*) Pupils are to be instructed in the use of tools and the care of tools, particularly agricultural implements and chiefly those requiring horses.

(*e*) Pupils have to tend the domestic animals on the farms, under the supervision and direction of the teachers, and participate in all ordinary farm work in order to learn practical methods likely to be of use to farmers.

(*f*) Pupils may be sent to other farms to learn practical farming. Travelling expenses are to be paid by the State. Exemption may be granted from the practical courses to students who are sorely needed to work at their home farms. Such students to undergo examinations as others.

(*g*) Carpentry, blacksmithing, concrete making, music, gymnastics and drawing are also to be taught.

(*h*) A regulation for the schools is to be issued.

8. Pupils get free board, lodging and laundry for their work on the farms during the last two terms. A 100 kronur ($15.00) subsidy, from the State, to buy books is granted each pupil for the last term.

9. Yearly examinations and final examinations are held by the school.

10. Pupils, who pay their board, pay only cost price. Opportunity for collective boarding is to be provided.

11. Extensions may be held for farmers during terms. Other extensions: the inspectors of the cattle industry and for those supervisors of feeds each farmer must have for his stock.

12. The Minister of Agriculture has charge of supervision of the schools.

13. All costs for establishing the schools are to be borne by the State. This law went into effect October 15, 1938.

HORTICULTURE SCHOOL

In 1937 the State Horticulture School was established by an act of the Althing under the sponsorship of Einar Helgason, one of the outstanding horticulturists of Iceland and a member of the Althing. Einar Helgason received his degree in Botany and Agriculture from the University of Copenhagen.

The school was formally opened in 1939 and is located at Hveragerdir in Olfus. This district has many hot springs and many greenhouses have been built there. The school has a two-year course. Teaching and lodging are free.

The purpose of this school is to train young men for gardening and the operation of greenhouses, which is Iceland's source of home-grown vegetables. The school has three teachers who were trained at the University of Copenhagen. Two of the instructors specialized in horticulture and one in agriculture.

The school is wholly financed by the State and twelve students are allowed to attend each year. The students selected to attend this school must finish the elementary school, and must have taken the district school examination and must have done practical gardening for at least a year.

The course of study is divided between theory and practical work. Botany is the main theory course. The majority of the time is spent in the greenhouses getting practical knowledge.

The construction of new greenhouses in Iceland has been greatly accelerated since 1940. The critical "fresh vegetable" problem will be relieved to a certain extent by production from the greenhouses. Approximately eighty tons of tomatoes were produced in hothouses in 1942. This field of production, as it is expanding, will demand a new, revised and specialized education.

MUSIC SCHOOL

In 1931 a group of men, all musicians, interested in furthering Iceland's musical talent, founded a School of Music. Ragnar Jonson, Olafur Torgrimsson, Bjorn Jonson, led by Pall Isolfsson, were the men directly responsible for the school. The headmaster, Pall Isolfsson, is a professional organist and received his musical training in Germany. The school offers instruction in violin, cello, piano and flute. No voice training is given. Other courses required by the school are theory of music and musical history.

This school receives small grants from the State, but the majority of the funds come from recitals given throughout the school year by the Music Society of Iceland. Members of the Music Society can attend the recitals free.

The school has five instructors; all have received training abroad. The students range in age from 8 years to 30 years. The student pays 350 kronur ($52.50) per year fees. The school term lasts from October to April. This school is not connected with the grammar school or the university.

HANDICRAFT AND ARTS SCHOOL

One of the newest schools was started through private efforts of individuals wishing to forward education for those who will

Exhibits from the Arts and Handicraft School

make their homes in the rural areas. This school is the Handicrafts and Arts School, founded in January, 1940, by Ludwig Gudmundsson. The school had its beginning in a basement and offered woodwork, metal work, bookbinding and elementary drawing. At this time it had one teacher, Kurt Zier. To-day the staff has fourteen instructors. In October, 1941, the Arts Section was added.

The majority of the handicraft work is done by hand tools. The carving work, or Sloyd work, is based on Icelandic legends portrayed in the intricate patterns. The metal work consists of the making and repairing of small articles such as cooking utensils, candlesticks and bowls; repair of farm tools; and the making of horseshoes and harness. Students may enrol in this handicraft section at the age of sixteen. Those enrolling in the Arts Section must be at least sixteen and with art ability.

The headmaster of this school is Ludwig Gudmundsson who, in addition to being headmaster, is Chairman of the Information Centre of the University of Iceland for the use of students going abroad to educational institutions.

The Handicraft and Arts School is organized as follows:

Section A: *Teachers' Section*

The purpose of this section is to give prospective teacher special instruction in handicrafts and drawing.

I. *Training Section for Elementary Teachers.*

Requirements: The student must be eighteen years of age, of good health, of good character and have completed the elementary grades. Students entering this section are on probation for eight weeks before becoming regular students.

(a) The subjects offered in this section are:

1. Handicrafts for elementary grades. The construction of simple household furniture and carving (Sloyd) work.

2. Cardboard work such as the making of stationery portfolios and cardboard boxes of various kinds for use about the home.

3. Drawing (freehand) of popular national patterns.

4. Handicrafts for small children in the primary grades.

This section may be completed in one year, or the student may take two years to complete the subjects.

II. *Training Section for Teachers in District Schools.*
   This is a two-year course.
   (*a*) Handicrafts for elementary grades.
   (*b*) Cardboard work.
   (*c*) Drawing.
   (*d*) Handicrafts.
       (All the above are the same as in the former section.)
   (*e*) Leatherworking.
   (*f*) Bookbinding.
   (*g*) Concrete work.
   (*h*) The making of hand puppets and their operation.
   (*i*) Icelandic.
   (*j*) Science of teaching and the history of education.
   (*k*) Hygiene.

The last three courses are taken at the Teachers' Training School for regular teachers in the elementary school.

III. *Teachers' Training Section for Drawing Teachers in Elementary and District Schools.*
   This is a two-year course for elementary teachers and a three-year course for district school teachers.
   (*a*) Drawing, freehand, of common objects and anatomy.
   (*b*) Painting. Still life, landscape and picture composition.
   (*c*) Graphics, woodcuts and etchings.
   (*d*) Applied arts, decorative patterns and designs.

In all these divisions of the Teacher Training Sections the Handicraft and Arts School conducts practice teaching for prospective teachers. The courses and school have no fees. Students pay for materials only. Each student must work two hours weekly for the school. The school day consists of eight hours.

IV. *Teachers' Training Section for students of the Icelandic Teachers' Training School of regular elementary school teachers.*
   This section gives students in the regular Teachers' Training School an opportunity to take courses of their selection in order to gain knowledge and skills in handicrafts in addition to their regular courses.

Exhibition at the end of the year of the students' work in the Arts
and Handicraft School

V. *Short Courses for Teachers already in service.*

These courses may run one or two weeks and may offer courses in:

(*a*) Chalk drawing on blackboards.

(*b*) Metal work.

(*c*) Picture making for primary grades.

(*d*) Handicrafts for young children.

SECTION B: *Arts Section*

The purpose of this section is to give instruction in drawing, painting and graphics.

The requirements for entrance are to be at least sixteen years of age and exhibit art ability in the form of drawings or paintings.

The subjects offered in this section are:

(*a*) Drawing, freehand, of common objects and anatomy.

(*b*) Painting. Still life, landscape and picture composition.

(*c*) Graphics, woodcuts and etchings.

(*d*) Applied art, decorative patterns and designs.

If a student so desires he may take only one of the above subjects or the entire course.

SECTION C: *For Crippled People*

The purpose of this section is to train crippled people in certain handicrafts.

Training is given in bookbinding and leatherworking.

SECTION D: *Evening Class*

The purpose of this section is to give working people or those students in other schools an opportunity to get instruction in handicrafts and arts. Students in this section must pay a tuition fee. The courses in this section are:

(*a*) Drawing class for children 7 to 10 years, and 11 to 14 years of age.

(*b*) Woodworking class for children 7 to 10, and 11 to 14 years of age.

(*c*) Leatherworking for adults.

(*d*) Drawing and painting class for all persons who care to attend.

(*e*) Bookbinding for Boy Scouts.
Bookbinding for students of the university.
Bookbinding for all other persons who care to attend.

(f) Wood carving.

(g) Furniture design and drawing class.

(h) Painting, colour mixing and application.

Section E: *Farm Training*

This is a proposed section that will soon be started for those students coming from rural areas. This section will give training in metal work and furniture construction.

SCHOOL FOR DEAF AND DUMB CHILDREN

With an increasing population and added educational facilities the necessity for a school for deaf-mute children soon presented itself. In 1904 a school for deaf-mute children was established in Reykjavik with a division for mental defectives.

This school, however, had its beginning abour 1890 when the clergyman, Reverend Pall Palsson, started a private school for those children with speech impediments. The Reverend Palsson was afflicted with stammering and went to Copenhagen for treatment and was cured; upon his return to Iceland he began his own private school for those unfortunate children with the same trouble.

To-day the school for deaf-mute children is a boarding school and is usually attended by approximately thirty pupils from various parts of the country. This school is wholly maintained by the State. It has three teachers.

In 1922 the Althing passed a law concerning the school which stated as follows:

1. Parents and guardians must send their deaf and dumb children to this school each fall when they reach the age of 8 years, unless the parents prove before the educational authorities that such handicapped children are receiving adequate instruction at home. The children are to stay in this school until they are seventeen years of age unless they graduate sooner.

2. Parents and guardians are to pay for travelling expenses to and from the school and for all necessary clothing for the child. If the parents are poor the State pays expenses. Room and board is to be paid by parents or guardian if possible. However, the State in all cases pays one-third of all expenses.

3. During the summer these children, whose parents or guardians can afford it, are allowed to go home; other children remain at the school or places are found for them during the summer months. The State pays half of such travelling cost.

4.   Upon completion of the school in cases where the parents are dead the steward of the school finds a place for the young person to go.

5.   The educational authorities issue rules concerning courses of study and other matters pertaining to the school.

6.   If money is available the school accepts those children with defective speech, the hard of hearing and feeble-minded.

In 1933 a school for blind children and adults was established by Blindravinafelag Islands (The Society of Blind People). This school is located in Reykjavik and is maintained by the State.   It is the only one in the country.   The Braille system is used to teach elementary subjects.   The school has one teacher. An average of 25 people attend each year.   The students are trained to do handiwork such as basket making, chairs and mats. They also learn weaving and sewing.   This handiwork is sold and the money given to the blind people.

The people attending this school range from ten to thirty years of age.

PART IV

TEACHERS' UNION FOR ELEMENTARY SCHOOL TEACHERS

Through the years the teachers of Iceland struggled against odds and fought their battles individually. It was in 1889 that the first teachers' society was founded. Its purpose was to better teaching conditions and school opportunities. This Teachers' Society has now grown and developed into the Teachers' Union for Elementary School Teachers. This union champions vigorously the causes of the teachers of the country. All teachers are required to belong, and the annual fee is 10 kronur ($1.50).

Each school district or town sends representatives to the annual meeting. This annual meeting drafts proposals to be submitted to the Ministry of Education or directly to the Parliament.

It can be said that the direct result of this union of teachers has been the recognition of teachers' rights as to pay, tenure of office, working conditions and the betterment of school opportunities and facilities for the children of the country.

The main objective of the union at the present time is a planned building programme for the next few years. It is planned to have a school building in every district to accommodate the children of that district at present, and allow for any expansion in the near future.

Recently, through the efforts of the union, the teachers received a 1,000 kronur ($150.00) per year increase in salary.

To keep all members of the union informed as to current events the magazine *Menntamal*, their official organ, is issued.

In 1924 the educational periodical for teachers, *Menntamal*, became the strong official organ for all teachers of Iceland. However, other periodicals were started as early as 1888, the first being *Timarit um appeldi og Menntamal*, a periodical on instruction and education. It was edited by Jon Thorarinsson and lasted five years. Others from time to time came into being under different names until 1935 when *Mentnamal* was purchased by the Union of Icelandic Elementary School Teachers.

This magazine is printed quarterly and carries all information that has to do with modern teaching trends, articles concerning deceased members of the profession, letters of information from other parts of the country, book reviews, current events, surveys, petitions to the Althing and general news of members of the Teachers' Union.

"Reykholtsskoli"

An elementary school in the country. The site of the school was the home of Snorri Sturluson

It can be said that the Teachers' Union shapes the thoughts of the teachers of the country and with unremitting effort has become a powerful force for the teachers' and for school children's rights and privileges.

RECENT TRENDS IN ELEMENTARY SCHOOLS

SUPERVISORS

Supervisors of elementary schools are being introduced, there being four in the elementary school system at the present time. Jakob Kristinsson, Director of Public Education, introduced the idea. Their chief objectives are:

1. To bring new methods to the rural schools.
2. To create better relations between the county finance committee and the boards of education.

The men selected for these supervisory jobs are former teachers and men well-grounded in school finance and the problems of the rural schools.

SWIMMING

The elementary schools in the larger towns where swimming pools are available have introduced and stress swimming. This is a required subject, and certain requirements must be met by boys and girls to get a certificate in the course. The requirements are as follows:

The youngest student must swim ten yards.

The next examination required upon leaving the elementary school of both boys and girls is:

Swim thirty yards, using the breast stroke.
Swim fifteen yards, using back stroke.
Swim twenty yards in clothing.
Be able to dive and know about life-saving.

The (b) part of the examination is as follows:
Swim one hundred yards, using breast stroke.
Swim forty yards, using back stroke.
Swim twenty-five yards in clothing.
Swim twenty yards, pulling person of equal size.
Be able to dive one and one-half yards down.
Know artificial respiration.

The following is required for students upon leaving the Nautical or Marine Engineers' Schools:
Swim two hundred yards, using the breast stroke.
Swim fifty yards, using the back stroke.
Swim fifteen yards under the water.

Swim fifty yards in clothing.
Swim twenty-five yards with a person of equal size.
Dive one and one-half to two and one-half yards down.
Be able to break holds of drowning persons and know artificial respiration.

If a student wishes he or she may pass the following examination in swimming:
Swim one thousand yards, using the breast stroke, in:
    Twenty-two minutes for boys.
    Thirty minutes for girls.
Swim one hundred yards, using breast stroke, in one minute, and
    Thirty-five seconds for boys.
    Fifty seconds for girls.
Swim one hundred yards, using the back stroke.
Swim fifty yards, using the crawl stroke.
Swim twenty-five yards with an equal-sized person both in clothing.
Undress while swimming.
Know artificial respiration and life-saving.

One can easily see the value of such training as this in a country entirely surrounded by the Atlantic ocean and its main source of income derived from the fishing industry.

VISUAL EDUCATION

Visual education by means of motion pictures is one of the more recent progressive measures introduced into the Icelandic schools. Far-sighted school authorities here have realized that modern educational methods must be employed to illustrate processes, situations and modes of living.

Motion pictures made their first appearance in Icelandic classrooms in 1930 when one of the headmasters of the Co-educational Secondary School at Reykjavik introduced them. The idea of visual education first came from the University of Copenhagen.

To-day approximately 20 elementary and secondary schools use film for instructional purposes. Geography and the natural sciences have been stressed most in the films. New films of the industries and farming in Iceland are being added.

Visual education has received some financial support from the Government. Part of the proceeds from an entertainment tax is used to increase the film library.

Under the progressive guidance of its director, Jakob Kristins-son, the Icelandic public school system now has two portable projectors and a library of 60 films in circulation. At the beginning of the 1943–44 school term they will have twenty projectors. One of the problems to be overcome in the rural districts is the lack of electrical power to run the projectors in the schools.

Educators and civic groups in Iceland are becoming increasingly interested in presenting to school children visual facts about their country, its industries and community life. This interest has become more intense since the occupation of the country by Allied Armies. Iceland must be presented in an interesting fashion to keep the younger generation nationalistic and interested in their homeland.

The University of Iceland, a young institution, also has a programme of visual education. It operates a motion picture house in Reykjavik and uses it in a dual rôle. This show house competes commercially with other theatres as well as showing instructional and cultural films for the student body.

OFFICE OF INFORMATION
ON FOREIGN EDUCATIONAL INSTITUTIONS

In 1920 the university student body elected its first student council. One year later the student council founded the Office of Information. One of the members of this early council was not only a serious student but was interested in helping others in the university go abroad for further study. Ludwig Gudmundsson had, from 1917 to 1920, visited countries and universities on the Continent. Upon his return to Iceland he entered the university with a great knowledge of other educational institutions. He has lost none of his zeal for furthering his fellow countrymen's hunger for knowledge. He was the driving force in starting the present-day Information Office. Most Icelandic students going abroad for further study are aided by this office.

This office works in co-operation with the American-Scandinavian Foundation, an American institution dedicated to promote better intellectual relations between the United States, Sweden, Denmark, Iceland and Norway by means of an exchange of students, publications and a Bureau of Information.

Icelandic students desiring to go to any foreign university or institution of higher learning contact the Office of Information which has the necessary catalogues and information. The Office of Information also helps the student secure visa, passport, etc. A student going to the United States gets a letter of introduction from the Icelandic-American Society to the American-Scandinavian Foundation Chapter nearest where he is to be a student. This aids him in getting established in his new home.

G

After the student has entered the foreign educational institution he is still in contact with the Office of Information which maintains complete and up-to-date records on all students in foreign universities.

During the past ten years over 900 Icelandic students have studied abroad. Before the war the majority of students were in schools in the following countries in the order named: Denmark, Germany, Sweden, Norway, England, France and the United States, with only a very few in other countries. Since the beginning of the war students are going to the United States and Great Britain. During 1942 students were located as follows:

1.	Denmark ..	.. ..	150
2.	United States	.. ..	96
3.	Sweden ..	.. ..	25
4.	Norway ..	.. ..	18
5.	England ..	.. ..	15
6.	Germany ..	.. ..	15
7.	Canada ..	.. ..	13
8.	Scotland ..	.. ..	4

Icelandic university students studying abroad have attended the following universities and technological institutes:

1. Denmark	Copenhagen, University of Aarhus, University of
2. Norway	Oslo, University of, and Norway's Technological Institute (Norges teknishehojskole in Trondhjem)
3. Sweden	Stockholm, University of Lund, University of Uppsala, University of
4. Germany	Berlin, University of, and Berlin Technological Institute (Technische Hochscule) Munich, Technological Institute Leipzig, University of Dresden, Technological Institute Cologne, University of
5. Austria	Vienna, University of
6. France	Paris, Sorbonne Grenoble
7. Great Britain	London Edinburgh Glasgow Leeds

8. United States   Minnesota, University of
                    Illinois, University of
                    California, University of
                    Iowa, University of
                    Wisconsin, University of
                    Michigan, University of
                    Johns Hopkins University
                    New York University
                    University of Washington
                    Baylor University
                    Boston School of Dentistry
                    Rensselaer Polytechnical Institute
                    Cornell University
                    University of Southern California
9. Canada   University of Manitoba
                    McGill University, Montreal
                    University of Toronto

Before 1933 forty-six Icelandic university students were in Germany and twenty-eight in Denmark. In 1938–39 seventy-three Icelandic students were in Denmark and only twenty-two in Germany. A marked rise of students in other Scandinavian countries was noted after 1933.

It is difficult to narrow down the field of study to a particular branch or subject. Icelandic students have gone into all fields of study. However, it may be said that more have studied engineering, natural history, dentistry, art, literature, philology, history, philosophy and education than any of the various other fields.

The Office of Information for Icelandic students going abroad to study is indeed serving its purpose well. Detailed correspondence between the office and the institution in which the student is matriculated is in progress at all times concerning the progress of the student. To further aid the student an Icelandic-American Society was founded in 1940 in order to insure closer working relations with the American-Scandinavian Foundation. In fact, the Icelandic-American Society is set up along the same lines as the Foundation.

Since its beginning the Office of Information for Icelandic students has aided more than a thousand students, and is expanding each year.

THE CULTURE FUND

In 1928 the Althing passed a law for a fund to be established by the name of "Menningarsjothur," or Culture Fund. This fund had for its objects the furtherance of general learning in the country, provision for research into the natural resources of Iceland, promotion of the growth of national arts and provision for funds for scholarships for students going abroad to obtain higher degrees.

The income of the fund is from proceeds from the sale of wines and spirits which have been illegally smuggled into the country and confiscated by the public prosecutor, the proceeds of the sale of ships, foreign or domestic, confiscated under similar circumstances and all fines for infringements of the liquor law. Both the law itself and regulations concerning it.

This fund is under the supervision of the Culture Board which is charged with furthering the culture of the country as a whole. In April of each year the board divides the income from the preceding year into three even parts.

(a) One-third is set aside for use in publishing good native or translated works for general good and selected poetry and fiction.

(b) One-third for use for scientific research of the country's natural resources and for publishing essays and treatises on the same.

(c) One-third for use in buying objects of art for the State and giving prizes for plans of buildings, furniture and models of home handicraft. Also reproductions of works of Icelandic art for indoor decoration.

Parts of the fund may be used for the Building of Natural Science and for the Art Museum. The selection and direction of the public works is done by a committee of three, which is as follows:

(a) Two professors of literature from the university and one teacher of Icelandic from the Teachers' Training School.

(b) The part used for research under the direction of three, the Director of the Natural Science Museum and two teachers of natural science in the grammar schools. One to be from Reykjavik and one from Akureyri.

(c) The part to further arts is under the direct control of the culture board.

If this fund in any year exceeds a mean income two-thirds of the surplus is set aside for buildings mentioned in regulation two, Art Museums. The funds to be deposited in the National Bank and the Althing directs disposition, one-third of surplus is used to publish outstanding books that would be too costly to publish by the yearly income going to the individual. The culture board can appoint a man to transact business in connection with the selling of published works. Members of the board must not sit in deciding their own works. The department furthering Icelandic Art must deal in works of painting and sculpture, evenly divided. This Culture Fund has 50,000 kronur ($7,500.00) yearly.

THE CULTURE BOARD

This board has administrative power over the Culture Fund and the provisions of the law creating such a fund.

1. Each new Althing elects a board of five members, and any Icelandic citizen living in Reykjavik or nearby is eligible to be a member. The pay is 600 kronur ($90.00) per year.

2. Object or purpose of the board is to:
   (a) Allocate yearly sum granted by Althing to poets and artists.
   (b) Buy objects of art of Icelandic origin.
   (c) Supervise the Art Museum and prepare plans for buildings.
   (d) Sanction plans for building of new churches and for the alteration of the old ones; to select location of churches.
   (e) Allocate scholarships as granted by the State to regular and special students. The board is guided in the selection of these students by what is most necessary for the country. The ability and character of the individual is considered. The Culture Board, as far as possible, sees that students use their grant well and properly. If not used properly the grant may be rescinded.
   (f) Make free ship passage allocation to those going abroad to study.
   (g) Supervise fund that may be established by law for furtherance of arts and schools if instructed to do so.

MINISTRY OF EDUCATION

In 1904 the Ministry of Education was created and made a part of the duties of the Minister of Churches. This ministry was known as the Ministry of Schools and Churches.

Only a year before the Minister of Icelandic Affairs was a Dane residing in Copenhagen and was not responsible to the Althing. However, the Icelandic constitution was amended and an Icelander was to be Minister of the country's affairs and was to reside in Reykjavik. And since then all the affairs of the country have been in the hands of the Icelanders themselves.

EXAMINATIONS

Examinations are very important in the schools of Iceland. They act as a sifting process in that only the best go on to the higher education. Secondly, the rigid examinations give the student a feeling of accomplishing something worthwhile.

The headmasters and school boards of the elementary schools make up the examinations. In order for the student to graduate from the elementary school he must take this examination. The school board appoints one person who is not a teacher to attend the examination and mark the students and judge them to enter the next higher school or class. The examinations are both written and oral.

In the Secondary or Latin Schools the teachers and a censor appointed by the Minister of Education give the marks to the student passing from one class to another, or from one division to the next higher division. It is highly competitive in gaining the Latin or Grammar School, and examinations are usually given in May of each year, allowing the student to enter the school the following September. As a rule tutors are employed to prepare students for the Grammar School examinations. This tutoring is usually done by the regular secondary teachers in their free time, which practice is allowed by school authorities.

The Rector of the secondary schools makes up the entrance examination. The number of students allowed to enter the Grammar Schools is limited. The reason being that too many would be trained for professional jobs and not enough trained for manual jobs.

This is an example of the leaving examination for the Grammar Schools:

A student of the Grammar School is tested in the following:
Icelandic
    written; important years in Iceland, about the fate of Norway, and about rain.
Danish
English
    written; translation of English to Icelandic, about 25 lines.
German
    translation Icelandic to German.
French
    oral.
Latin
    translate from Cicero to Icelandic and translate Icelandic to Latin.

Mathematics
square root and algebraic formula, geometry and trigonometry.

The reason for oral examinations is to find the student's depth
of knowledge of subjects as well as related information.

TEACHERS' SALARIES AND PENSIONS

The Icelandic teacher is underpaid. The average pay of the
elementary school teacher is 300 kronur ($45.00) per month.
This is the pre-war salary. Elementary teachers are not paid
during the summer months but must augment their salaries by
working on farms, for the State in road construction, or in surveying the country. The average pay of the secondary or grammar
school teacher is 4,500 to 5,000 kronur ($675.00 to $750.00) per
year, with a raise every fifth year. However, this income is
supplemented by tutoring students during the teachers' free time.
In the university the beginning professor gets 4,500 kronur
($675.00) per year, plus a 2,000 kronur ($300.00) bonus each
year. The Althing made the bonus available due to low salary.
Because of the rising cost of living due to the war an increase of
seventy-five per cent. is given the university instructors. For
each three years' service the university instructor gets a 500
kronur (75.00) increase until they reach 6,000 kronur ($900.00)
per year. In this manner a university instructor will reach the
maximum salary at the end of nine years' service. A teacher
getting 6,000 kronur ($900.00) per year salary thus would be
getting 12,500 kronur ($1,875.00) per year during the war.

The Rector of the University receives the same salary plus
bonus as do any of the other instructors, with, however, a 2,000
kronur ($300.00) expense fund per year. This expense fund is
made to the Rector for the purpose of accepting and entertaining
visiting professors.

The newly appointed Field Supervisors of schools receive
20,000 kronur ($3,000.00) per year, or approximately that. The
reason for this higher salary is due to the high cost of travelling
about the country.

When teachers reach the age of sixty-five they must retire.
A pension plan was started in 1919. In order to have a pension
fund seven per cent. of the yearly salary of teachers is put aside.
Upon arrival at the retirement age these teachers are allowed to
draw from this pension fund twenty-five one-thousandths of
their salary at the time of retirement. The top pension is 75
per cent. of salary. Thus the amount a retired teacher draws
is dependent upon the number of years he has paid into the pension

fund up to seventy-five per cent. of his salary during working years.

PUBLIC EXPENDITURE FOR ELEMENTARY EDUCATION

According to a recent report from the Director of Public Education, J. Kristinsson, more than 3,000,000 kronur ($450,000.00) has been spent on public education in Iceland during the year 1941 and a similar amount will be spent in 1942. This amounts to a little over 30 kronur ($4.50) per person, which is expended for educational purposes.

When it is considered that the population of Iceland is a little over one hundred and thirty thousand people this is by no means a small amount of money. It is a fairly good index of the work performed for general education of the people.

The Ministry of Education has just lately appointed four supervisors of schools. Their job is to travel around their respective territories and observe the conditions existing in the schools, aid the teachers in their work and suggest improvements where they are needed.

This is undoubtedly a progressive step, and it is to be hoped that this arrangement will lead to greater and more important improvements in the educational system of Iceland. Money spent on education of children, who are the hope of the future, is not thrown into the sea, as J. Kristinsson has rightly stated. "Some may think the amount spent on public education is more than enough without being increased, but it is the happiness and well-being of our younger generation which is at stake, and nothing is too good for its benefit."

PROGRESS IN METHODS AND EQUIPMENT

The structure of everyday life in Iceland before 1939 has already been profoundly modified, specially in the cities. Country life, habits and customs remain the same. Iceland must gear itself to the fact that when this war is over geographical barriers will disappear. It, after many years of isolation, is being forced to take a world viewpoint.

The younger generation will deviate from old ties due to their coming in contact with other peoples in and from many countries. The young Icelander has a rich heritage, one of the richest in the world. He must not be allowed to put this rich heritage in a corner and forget about it, nor allow it to be replaced by newer and superficial things.

With the turning point of the old and new conflict at hand the educational authorities of the country feel that the time has come for a reorganization as to means and methods, that is, to dramatize the old Sagas, animate them, make them live in a modern world in such a manner that the new generation will know and remember them.

The modern methods of psychology and instruction are rather like the old Icelandic ways of teaching. The present-day schools are mostly based on Danish and English methods. The culture of Iceland is much older than the means of imparting it, in fact the elementary schools are very young, dating from about 1900. Prior to this time the instruction for the children was done in the home during the long winter evenings when the head of the household told and read the Sagas and, in a sense, lectured on their good points and pointed to the strong appeal of them. This was the theoretical part of the instruction. The practical part was gained by actual work on the land. They made their own cloths and machinery.

In order to have a good foundation for this reorganization the outstanding educators of the country are bending their efforts towards setting up an experimental school with the most able teachers in the country. In this experimental school there would be equipment fitted to the Icelanders and their surroundings. In other words, fit the instruction to the Icelandic surroundings as they are to-day.

Upon this controlled research would be written the textbooks needed for the new instruction. Different levels of ability would be established and carried out to all schools, and teachers would fit instruction to these ability levels. Tests would be devised and put into use. This experiment would cover a period of five to six years.

Now after the modern psychological methods are applied to the rich literature and culture of the past a still greater problem faces the educators of the country. What of the old to keep and build up and what to discard? Obviously the best from each century would be the solution; a selection of the old literature well written and illustrated and dramatized, to make them interesting for the youngsters, would make this history live.

This change will call for action on the part of the administrators of the country to-day. The following things would have to be done:

1. More advanced and detailed instruction of teachers.
2. Better pay for the teachers, thus making it possible for them to spend more time in better preparing themselves for their life work.

3. More and larger school buildings and additional class-room equipment.

The oldsters believe in the old things and wish to hold them and keep them a part of life, but they are failing to take any steps to make the old things interesting and a part of the life of the youngsters.

CONCLUSION

In reading these pages one may see that the picture of education and its growth in Iceland is clear and unforgettable. The bad times helped the nation to prove that it could rise and meet emergencies.

The Icelandic people, through struggle and great sacrifice, have created a school system which suits them as a free and democratic people. The right foundation, freedom of spirit, was laid centuries ago and has been followed down through the years.

The most regulating factor of Icelandic schools and culture has been the language of the country. Prior to the 18th century probably the most developed languages in the world were Greek, Latin and Icelandic. The most remarkable thing about the language is the fact that the beginning child in school to-day can read the Icelandic written 1,000 years ago. The change during this period of time has been negligible.

The language has had a political influence upon the country. During the Danish rule much Danish influence crept into it. In throwing off this influence the Icelandic peoples were gradually working for independence.

Next to the language the Sagas are most important as an influence on schools, education and culture of the country. Due to the isolation of the country the Sagas have had great influence, both past and present. In the past they were the guiding light of the people; to-day they are the historical importance of the country. These Sagas are quoted to-day and still exert an influence on the life of the people. It would be difficult to find a native in Iceland who has not read and re-read these Sagas. Students are examined in them in the schools.

The next striking thing in Icelandic education, apparent in early times as well as at the present time, is memory work. In early years, due to lack of books and writing materials, much memory work was done. The people learned the Sagas by memory and they were passed on by word of mouth. An early means of education, also very characteristic of to-day, was the study of laws at the Althing, the reciting of poems, the study of genealogy and the reciting of the Sagas.

The fact that Iceland has stood for over 1,000 years without armed conflict with other nations is silent testimony of the country's stability. The people have the trait of being able to recover.

True to the Scandinavian tradition of freedom, the schools of Iceland are State-controlled and run. Even the few private schools are State-subsidized. In short, all of the people of the country have a voice in how the educational system is organized and operated.

The first seven years of education in Iceland is compulsory for all children of the country. Rich and poor alike attend the same schools. This is a great leavening process.

Decentralized control tends to give each community the best possible education for each sphere of life in each community or area of the country.

It can truthfully be stated that schools supported by a democratic State turn out young men and women consecrated to serve their fellow beings.

All teachers in Iceland are of the opinion that school work serves as an active apprenticeship to life rather than as an abstract preparation for it. The educators of this country believe that their job is to train the coming generation to be better and more intelligent farmers, tradesmen, business men and artists than their fathers, and thus build a better nation. The educational system of Iceland has resolved to tie its work to the nation's needs and background. The duty of the teachers will be to provide adequate preparation for new special responsibilities.

The educational leaders in the past relied on their own best judgment and inflexible conscience. The leaders of the present day are deeply interested in the advancement of education in Iceland and are willing to obtain a better educational system at a price. The present-day leaders in the educational field realize that the world of to-morrow will be a world with potentialities for human betterment.

Far-sighted management in the Icelandic schools of to-day assures better things to-morrow. The schools of Iceland have in the past trained its peoples to be good neighbours in a decent world community and will so continue in the future. Schools must bring their curriculum into intimate touch with the realities of the modern world. Hate usually follows in the wake of war, but it is certain a new and better world cannot be founded on hate; thus it is up to the teachers of every nation to mould a new generation with the realization that they must live in harmony with all other individuals. The schools have always given the Icelandic people an opportunity to become truly human.

Bibliography

1. *Lythmenntun* (Public Education), by G. Finnbogason.
2. *Aevisaga Jons Thorkellsson* (Autobiography of Jon Thorkellsson).
3. *Biskupasogur* (Histories of the Bishops).
4. *Sithbotin a Islandi* (The Reformation in Iceland), by Thorkell Bjarnsason.
5. *Islandssaga* (History of Iceland), by Bugi Th. Melsted.
6. *Saga Alpythumenntunar a Islandi* (The History of Public Education in Iceland), by Gunnar M. Magnuss.
7. Compilation of National Laws of Iceland.
8. *Saga Islendinga Seytjanda Old* (The History of Iceland in the 17th Century), by Pall Eggert Olason.
9. *Saga Island*, 1930, by Samuel Eggertsson.
10. *Islandische, Dichter Der Neuzeit*, by J. C. Poestion, 1897 (with a Summary of Mental Life in Iceland since the Reformation).
11. *Islenzk Menning*, by Sigurdur Nordal, 1942.
12. *Edda and Saga*, by Bertha S. Phillpotts, 1937.

Index

PERSONS MENTIONED

PLACES MENTIONED

Akranes, 38.
Akureyri, 6, 7, 39, 40, 42, 57, 84.
Alftanes, 21.
Bessastadir, 5, 20, 40.
Blondas, 4, 58.
Breifafjordur, 5.
Bremerholm, 26.
Eidar, 6, 69.
Eidum, 69.
Eyjafjardarsysla, 5.
Flatey Island, 5.
Gerdir in Gardur, 6.
Grimsnes, 7.
Grunnastadir, 6.
Hafnarfjordur, 6.
Haukadal, 1, 3, 14.
Haukodalur, 17.
Hausastadir, 5, 21.
Helgafell, 4, 17.
Hof Farm, 57.
Holar, 1, 2, 4, 5, 6, 7, 8, 13, 14, 16, 17, 19, 20, 39, 69.
Holavellir, 40.
Hrafnseyri, 22.
Hrutafjordur, 7.
Hunavatns, 5.
Hunavatnssysla, 57.
Hvanneyri, 69.
Hveragerdir, 7, 71.
Hvitarbakki, 6.
Isafjordur, 6, 25.
Kjalarnes, 21.

Laekjamot Farm, 57.
Modruvellir, 6.
Mulathing, 18.
Nordfjordur, 38.
Odda, 1, 14.
Olafsdal, 6, 69.
Olfus, 71.
Reykholt, 4, 15.
Reykir, 7.
Reykjavik, v, vii, 5, 6, 7, 17, 20, 21, 22, 27, 28, 29, 36, 37, 39, 40, 42, 44, 45, 50, 52, 53, 54, 57, 58, 60, 61, 67, 76, 77, 80, 81, 84, 85.
Seydisfjordur, 38.
Siglufjordur, 38.
Skaftafellssysla, 18.
Skagafjardar, 5.
Skagafjardarsysla, 57.
Skalholt, 2, 3, 4, 5, 8, 13, 14, 16, 17, 19, 20, 21, 39.
Solheimer, 7.
Stokkseyri, 6.
Thingeyjarthing, 18.
Thingeyri, 4.
Thingvellir, 3, 12, 13.
Undirfell Farm, 57.
Videy Island, 4, 17.
Westmann Isles, 5, 46.
Ytriey Farm, 57.

OTHER NAMES MENTIONED

Althing, 1, 6, 7, 13, 14, 23, 24, 26, 28, 29, 30, 31, 33, 34, 36, 38, 39, 43, 44, 45, 52, 57, 59, 60, 65, 68, 71, 76, 83, 84, 85, 87.
Althingishus (Aouse of Parliament, 44.
Arnemagnean Communion, 22.
Edda, 1, 2, 13, 14, 22, 45.
Fjolnir (periodical) 5, 23.
Fostodumadur (dean), 44.
Havamal (poem), 11.
Heimskringla, 2, 14.
Hemsard (book), 35.
Kennari (instructor), 44.
Kennslufraedi (course), 48.

Landshofding (governor), 27.
Landsspitals (State hospital), 44.
Menntamal (periodical), 7, 78.
Ny Felagsrit (periodical), 5, 24.
Orsted (system), 117.
Saga, 1, 11, 13, 21, 45, 89, 90.
Sigsdag (Danish Parliament), 27.
Sturlungasaga, 15.
Thorkillis Fund, 5, 21.
Uppeldisfraedi (course), 48.
Vigslodi (law book), 1.

BOOK CLUBS AND SOCIETIES

SCHOOLS

VOLCANOES